An Introduction to Personal Injury Law

DAVID S. BOYLE

boyle@deanscourt.co.uk
Deans Court Chambers
24 St. John Street
Manchester
M3 4DF

Law Brief Publishing

© David Boyle

All rights reserved. No part of this publication may be reproduced, stored in a retrieval system, or transmitted, in any form or by any means, electronic, mechanical, photocopying, recording or otherwise, without the prior permission of the publisher.

Excerpts from judgments and statutes are Crown copyright. Any Crown Copyright material is reproduced with the permission of the Controller of OPSI and the Queen's Printer for Scotland. Some quotations may be licensed under the terms of the Open Government Licence (http://www.nationalarchives.gov.uk/doc/open-government-licence/version/3).

Cover image © iStockphoto.com/photogl

The information in this book was believed to be correct at the time of writing. All content is for information purposes only and is not intended as legal advice. No liability is accepted by either the publisher or author for any errors or omissions (whether negligent or not) that it may contain. Professional advice should always be obtained before applying any information to particular circumstances.

Published 2017 by
Law Brief Publishing
30 The Parks
Minehead
Somerset
TA24 8BT

www.lawbriefpublishing.com

Paperback: 978-1-911035-30-5

To Estelle and Brian, my mum and dad,

who have always listened intently and nodded politely whenever I've blathered on about work. They had the point, way before it reached this level of distillation.

ACKNOWLEDGEMENTS

This book stems from Tim Kevan's enthusiasm for me writing something to transcend the niche areas of law which all too often define us once in practice. I thank both Tim and Garry Wright at Law Brief Publishing for their ongoing patience and cheerleading.

I was lucky enough to undertake pupillage with Craig Sephton QC (as he now is), who encouraged plain English, clear thinking and pointed advocacy. He told me that one cannot make bricks without straw, and couldn't possibly comment about what I did with the raw materials that he so generously provided.

This book is a reflection, and, I hope, a distillation, of all that I have learned from trying to explain things to others. They know who they are, even if it isn't fair to name them. Some are friends who, for whatever reason, suddenly needed an understanding of personal injury law on the off chance that they were asked a question beyond their existing expertise. Helen Rutherford and Gareth Poole were pupils who didn't have a say in the matter. Some were mini-pupils who only had a day or two to take on board all that I threw at them. Many were clients, trying to understand the state and merits of their case before making a decision which would affect the rest of their life. Their patience, or at least willingness to be talked at, has been an invaluable catalyst for the process. I bear in mind that a catalyst is unchanged by the experience. Some of them tell me that what I say is actually helpful, disqualifying themselves from the definition. I thank them all, irrespective of their status.

As with my previous book, I have enlisted the proof-reading assistance of my old, good, and non-lawyer friend, David Chart, whose thirst for knowledge of whatever type remains unabated, even if I always feel that I dilute his intellectual reservoir.

As ever, Carin, John, and my clerks have, in their own different ways, cajoled, encouraged, supported and tolerated, beyond the call of duty, the additional time that I've spent in front of the computer screen, 'working' but not working. I really am very grateful.

DSB
May 2017

AUTHOR'S NOTE

There are things that we know that we need to know, and there are things that we know that we don't need to know. But there are also things that we don't know that we need to know.

There are even things that we don't know that we don't need to know, although, perhaps, we should not spend too much time on those. I have tried to cover the first and third categories, whilst acknowledging matters which might fall to be considered elsewhere.

Ultimately, a book is not only finite, but limited. The decisions as to what rightly falls to be considered in an 'Introduction' and the opinions expressed are, as at 29 May 2017, mine and mine alone.

DSB

FOREWORD

Many years ago I eagerly opened "An Introduction to the Law of Restitution" written by my former tutor, Professor Peter Birks, now sadly deceased. Like many young lawyers I was seeking a quick fix on a particular area of law. As I dipped into it I was baffled by its complexity and brilliance. Since then I have been wary of any legal text book described as "An Introduction to…"

The potential reader need have no such fear in relation to this handy volume written by the experienced practitioner, David Boyle. In eighteen pithy and well written chapters Mr Boyle guides you through the essentials of personal injury litigation. He provides a very fine over-view of this important area of law which touches the lives of so many people. It is clearly the work of a barrister of many years' standing, one who is used to explaining in lucid terms, to professional and lay clients alike, the relevant underlying principles and the practical nuts and bolts of personal injury law. It is a book written in an attractive and conversational style and one which will be a splendid vade mecum for those seeking a true introduction to this field.

Stephen Stewart
May 2017

Contents

Introduction		1

Part One – The Basics   3

Chapter One	An Introduction to Personal Injury Litigation		5
	1.1	The rules of three	8
Chapter Two	The Parties		11
	2.1	Claimants and Litigation Friends	11
	2.2	Defendants and Insurers	11
	2.3	The Lawyers	13
Chapter Three	An Overview of the Litigation Process		17
	3.1	The Accident	17
	3.2	Reporting the accident	17
	3.3	Notifying the claim	18
	3.4	Response	19
	3.5	Expert evidence	19
	3.6	Supporting documentation	20
	3.7	Negotiations	21
	3.8	Issue of proceedings	22
	3.9	The Particulars of Claim	23
	3.10	Service	24
	3.11	Acknowledgement of Service	25
	3.12	Defence	25
	3.13	Reply	26
	3.14	Directions	26
	3.15	Tracking	26
	3.16	Disclosure and Inspection	27
	3.17	Witness statements	28
	3.18	Medical evidence	28
	3.19	Schedules and Counter-schedules	28
	3.20	Trial	29

Chapter Four	The Legal Matrix and the Law of Tort	33
	4.1 Duty of care	33
	4.2 Breach of duty	33
	4.3 Causation	34
	4.4 Loss	35
	4.5 Conclusion	36

Part Two – Road Traffic Accidents 37

Chapter Five	Insurance and the MIB	39
	5.1 Indemnified drivers	39
	5.2 Non-indemnified drivers	41
	5.3 Uninsured drivers	43
	5.4 Unidentified drivers	43
	5.5 Last resort	44
Chapter Six	The Legal Issues	47
	6.1 Duty of care	47
	6.2 Breach of duty	48
	6.3 Causation and contributory negligence	49
Chapter Seven	The Factual Issues	51
	7.1 The rear end shunt	51
	7.2 Parallel Cars	52
	7.3 Oncoming cars	52
	7.4 Vehicle exiting a side road	53
	7.5 Oncoming vehicle turning across the other vehicle's path	54
	7.6 Roundabouts	55
	7.7 Opening door of parked car	56
	7.8 Single vehicle accidents	57
	7.9 Conclusion	58

Part Three – Public Liability Claims · 59

Chapter Eight	The Legal Issues		61
	8.1 Occupiers' Liability Act 1957		61
	8.2 Occupiers' Liability Act 1984		63
	8.3 Defective Premises Act 1972		64
	8.4 Highways Act 1980		65
	8.5 Nuisance/negligence		67
	8.6 Transient defects		68
Chapter Nine	The Factual Issues		71
	9.1 Does a duty apply? If so, what duty?		71
	9.2 Is there a prima facie breach of duty?		71
	9.3 Does the defendant have a defence?		71
	9.4 Did the hazard cause the claimant's accident?		72
	9.5 Contributory negligence		72
	9.6 Conclusion		74

Part Four – Employers' Liability Claims · 75

Chapter Ten	The Legal Issues		77
	10.1 Accident or Disease?		77
	10.2 Employment		78
	10.3 Duty of Care		79
Chapter Eleven	The Factual Issues		87
	11.1 What happened?		87
	11.2 Does a duty apply? If so, what duty?		88
	11.3 Is there a prima facie breach of that duty?		88
	11.4 Does the defendant have a defence?		89
	11.5 What caused the claimant's accident? Was there contributory negligence?		89
	11.6 Disease claims		90
	11.7 Conclusion		91

Part Five – Limitation   93

Chapter Twelve	The Legal Issues	95
	12.1 Section 11	96
	12.2 Section 14	97
	12.3 Section 33	98
Chapter Thirteen	The Factual Issues	101

Part Six – Quantum Issues   105

Chapter Fourteen	General Damages	107
	14.1 Pain, Suffering and Loss of Amenity	107
	14.2 Loss of Congenial Employment	110
Chapter Fifteen	Special Damages: Past Losses	113
	15.1 Property damage	113
	15.2 Medical treatment costs	114
	15.3 Aids and Appliances	115
	15.4 Care and Assistance	115
	15.5 Services	116
	15.6 Interest	117
Chapter Sixteen	Special Damages: Future Losses	119
	16.1 Multiplier/Multiplicands	
	16.2 Loss of earnings	119
	16.3 Smith v Manchester	122
	16.4 Blamire	123
	16.5 Loss of Pension claims	124
	16.6 Aids and Appliances, Future Care and Services	125 125
	16.7 Accommodation claims	
	16.8 Accelerated receipt	125 126

Part Seven – Miscellaneous Issues   **127**

Chapter Seventeen Things We Need to Know That We Don't   129
                   Need to Know
            17.1 Interim payments   129
            17.2 Provisional damages   130
            17.3 Periodical Payments Orders   130
            17.4 The Compensation Recovery Unit   131
            17.5 Personal Injury Trusts   132
            17.6 Court Approval   133
            17.7 Investment of Awards   133

Chapter Eighteen   Things We Need to Know, but Probably   135
                   Don't Want To
            18.1 Costs, the past and the future   135

Conclusion   141

INTRODUCTION

There are two types of people – those who want to know why they're doing what they're doing and those who just want to do it. For the latter, basic instruction and repetition will get them to a standard, but not beyond. That's fine by them, because they gain their satisfaction from completing the task asked of them, and there is no shame in belonging to that group – life is undoubtedly simpler: Ignorance is bliss.

For the rest of us, that gap in our knowledge is a frustration, particularly when the people around us seem to know so very much more than we do. There is that sense that we should know more, particularly when we are new to the party. There is always that feeling that people who arrived before us know just a little bit more than we do, the shortcuts and the cheat modes. We, on the other hand, are imposters — late arrivals that have no right to be there — and, not being in the in-crowd, we will make mistakes and look foolish.

It is that Imposter Syndrome which this book seeks to address, not by teaching the reader everything that one might possibly learn in infinite detail, or by giving the reader the necessary case law to scrape by in an exam, but in giving, in one relatively short book, an overview of the big picture, with enough guidance as to how one might then consider the necessary points in optimal detail. It cannot, and does not, promise to cover every aspect of personal injury law that one might meet, whether as paralegal, trainee solicitor, litigant in person or visitor from some other field of practice. Rather, the hope is to provide a distillation of knowledge and experience to set out the legal and practical landscape of this area of law, in the hope that the reader might bring their academic study, their factual problem, their legal experience or simply their intelligence, and, seeing that bigger picture, might use this book as a map from which to plan their foray into this area of work. Notable absentees include fatal accident claims, accidents abroad, product liability and the specifics of costs and assessment, none of which could be said to be appropriate for an introduction.

The law is constantly changing. The Civil Procedure Rules 1998 are constantly being amended, as are the Practice Directions. I have tried to refer to the relevant parts of the rules using CPR*x* or PD*x* as appropriate, but this is not a substitute for looking at the rules if one actually needs them.

PART ONE

THE BASICS

CHAPTER ONE
AN INTRODUCTION
TO PERSONAL INJURY
LITIGATION

Personal injury law is ubiquitous. Whilst only a tiny fraction of day to day legal practice in this country, it differs markedly from other areas of law because those engaged in this sort of law often work on an industrial scale, even though most individual clients only have one claim and might reasonably hope to receive a bespoke service. The advent of cold calling, advertising, and publicity from, amongst other sources, the insurance industry itself, has ensured that people are more aware than ever of the possibility of claiming compensation for injuries suffered as a result of somebody else's wrongdoing.

The insurance industry, unsurprisingly, feels that such claims have gotten out of hand. They have lobbied long and hard to reduce the cost of meeting such claims and have sought to avoid certain types of claim altogether. The politics of personal injury litigation are, with one or two exceptions, outside the remit of this volume. It would, however, appear that the decision to rename Plaintiffs as Claimants, in the Woolf reforms of 1999, gave rise to an increased perception of 'Claims Culture' (whatever that might actually be).

Could it be that a simply linguistic shift put in place a new mind-set about the morality of an industry which seeks to compensate people who have suffered injury? The word plaintiff undoubtedly elicits more sympathy than its replacement and this may be an example of the law of unintended consequences.

In any event, the concept of personal injury law is a simple one: Somebody (the 'claimant') suffers an injury to the person because of the wrongful (or 'tortious') acts or omissions of somebody else (the 'defendant') and brings a claim against them seeking monetary compensation which, in general terms, is designed to put the claimant back in the position they would have been in but for the actions of the defendant.

Of course, compensation rarely achieves that goal. It is not like for like. In minor cases, it is more of a recognition of the inconvenience of suffering from short-lived symptoms[1], whilst in circumstances where there are permanent injuries (e.g. the loss of a limb) the money paid is not a magic wand, somehow undoing the injuries suffered. Given the choice between a cheque and going back to the pre-accident situation, most injured people would rather have the impossible. Lawyers are often accused of only being interested in money, but it is normally the only tool available.

Why is all this important? Society has, for many years, sought to protect its vulnerable citizens, providing a safety net for those who are injured, but that protection comes at a cost, and the resources of society are limited. A relatively low earner, whose financial contribution to society is predominantly to spend any salary received, is more easily compensated than the high earner, whose contribution extends not just to the income tax paid, but the jobs created, the salaries paid to others, the trade tariffs received by the government and so forth, but if somebody is injured and cannot work, there are significant ramifications, both for them and those around them, whatever their level of earnings and potential. If the person responsible can be identified and can be made to pay, why should the welfare state, which is designed as a safety net of last resort, have to pay instead?

Of course, the person responsible for causing the injury may not be in a position to make financial amends. Indeed, it is highly unlikely that he will be able to pay his victim's wages and other losses out of his own pocket. There is rarely any point in suing a 'man of straw', because the purpose of personal injury litigation is not to wreak vengeance upon the tortfeasor – it is to reach an end point where the claimant is compensated and, with any luck, the lawyers representing him will be paid. For those reasons, the existence of an insurance policy is often as significant as any other factor in personal injury litigation.

---

1 The cynic might add 'whether or not they were actually suffered'.

At this point, it is worth considering what it is that insurance actually does. Most people have come across home policies, motor policies or life policies. In each case, the insured party pays a sum of money (a 'premium') to the insurer for a policy of insurance which will pay out in the event that a specified type of event happens at some point in the future during the period for which the policy applies. That payment out can be a fixed amount, but is more normally an indemnity – a suitable sum to meet all liabilities which occur as a result of the event coming to fruition.

There has to be an element of chance to the risk coming to pass (one cannot insure against Friday happening next week) and it is, in effect, a bet, with the insurer taking the premium in the hope that it will not have to make payment. The very nature of the risk is uncertain, but there are normally risk factors which are well known to the insured and which the insurer has to factor in, in order to ensure that the deal being entered into a fair one. For those reasons, contracts of insurance are contracts of the utmost good faith – an insurer which takes the view that its insured has not been honest or has failed to declare a material fact will often withdraw indemnity under the policy. The effects of that withdrawal of indemnity differ depending on the type of policy in question and those matters are considered in the relevant chapters. What is or is not a material representation is beyond the scope of this book.

In some circumstances, the law requires an insurance policy to be taken out to cover certain risks. If one is driving a motor vehicle, there is a requirement under section 143 of the Road Traffic Act 1988 to hold a policy which will indemnify the driver against third party risks – his potential liability to another person arising from his negligent use of that motor car on the roads. The insured can go further, and take out a fully comprehensive policy which covers the losses which he might suffer as a result of his negligent driving, such as the repairs to his vehicle, but that is an option, rather than a legal requirement. Because the likely payout is greater (because two cars are potentially the subject of a claim for repairs rather than one), the premium is normally greater too. The other example of mandatory insurance is employers' liability insurance under the Employers' Liability (Compulsory Insurance) Act 1969.

Against that background, the law limits the circumstances in which such a claim can be made. It limits the types of harm which can be compensated. It limits who can bring a claim. It defines what does and does not constitute a 'tort' or wrong. It allows an injured person's compensation to be reduced for their own fault. It limits what an injured person can claim for, and it identifies, in certain circumstances, how much one might recover for a particular head of claim.

The existence of an insurance policy makes a personal injury claim a commercial transaction. Whatever each side feels about the merits of the case, the outcome is most likely to be an argument about the need to pay a sum of money and the appropriate amount.

That means that the two sides should approach personal injury litigation with straight-forward goals and rules in mind. These are my formulations of the respective raisons d'être of the two sides:

The rule of three for claimants[2]

A claimant wants to get as much as possible, as quickly as possible, with as little risk as possible, but cannot have all three. That analysis should form the basis of all decision-making from the claimant's perspective of the case, as long as one understands what is meant by risk. It is not merely the risk of losing and getting nothing, or failing to beat an offer. Whilst the word has negative connotations, risk is simply an element of uncertainty. Further evidence might clarify the future medical position for good or ill, but it reduces the risk, because the parties can be more certain of the outcome. Sometimes a decision has to be made at a point in time when the evidence is unclear. What is the effect of getting another scan? It might delay matters. It might show long-term deterioration which means that the case is worth more, or a lack of degenerative change which means that the case is worth less (albeit that that might be better news for the injured claimant). That is the 'risk' which has to be factored into the assessment, but for anybody advising a claimant, this

---

2 Invariably demonstrated by holding up the thumb, index and middle fingers of the left hand at right angles to each other and using the index finger of the right hand to draw a clockwise circle in the air above the finger tips.

starting point, with its visual reminder, remains an immensely useful tool.

The rule of three for defendants[3]

Defendants fight a case to trial for one or more of three reasons: To discourage the next claim, to resolve irreconcilable differences in the instant case, and/or a failure to appreciate that the case does not fall into one of the other two categories. From time to time somebody points out that cases sometimes fight because 'the solicitors hate each other' but, viewed closely, that tends to be a situation where both sides want to put down a marker for the next claim, their differences therefore become irreconcilable and they each then fail to realise that the case should be settled before trial, a combination of all three.

It is, of course, worth noting that whilst claimants tend to be individuals, invested in the outcome of the litigation because they have one chance to get the right result, defendants are normally represented by solicitors instructed by the insurance company. They have assessed the potential cost of the case, both in terms of damages which might be payable and the costs which both sides might incur. They are looking at the extent to which they can save on those potential liabilities. There is normally less emotion, not because the defendant is any less invested in the litigation process, but because, for the most part, the defendant has already reached the conclusion that personal injury litigation is a commercial transaction – a realisation which is harder to reach when one has suffered a potentially life-changing event.

---

3 As above, with the hands swapped.

CHAPTER TWO
THE PARTIES

Having identified the basic purpose of litigation, it is worth considering who might engage in the process.

Claimants and Litigation Friends

As a general rule, personal injury litigation is between a claimant (the person injured) and a defendant (the person who caused that injury), but there is no reason why two or more claimants might not bring their claims together if they arise out of the same facts: Indeed, there are more often good reasons to bring one action, because there are cost savings and the claims are often mutually supportive. This scenario often arises where an entire family is involved in an accident, all suffering some injury or another.

Importantly, it is worth noting at this point that a claimant cannot bring an action in their own name if they lack capacity in law. That means that a claimant who has not reached the age of majority (18 in the UK) cannot bring a claim without a 'Litigation Friend' – a responsible adult, normally a close relative – who can give instructions to the lawyers and take steps within the proceedings. CPR21 applies.

The same applies to claimants who have reached the age of 18, but do not have capacity, either because they never had it, or because they have lost it as a result of the accident (or some other supervening event). In cases where a claimant has suffered a head injury, or has developed unrelated dementia, there may be no prospect of them ever regaining capacity to litigate the matter in their own name, but it is also possible to lose capacity on a temporary basis (e.g. where a claimant develops an opiate addiction because of their use of painkillers after the accident – they may temporarily lose their capacity until such time as they have their addiction under control). The nuances of the Mental Capacity Act 2005 warrant a separate volume but the primary principles of the Act are that a claimant is assumed to have capacity and should be helped to make their own decisions, wise or otherwise, if at all practicable. If and only if the claimant cannot make a decision should his rights and freedom of action be restricted. A light touch is required.

Where a claimant proceeds with a litigation friend, any settlement which might affect them has to be considered and approved by the court, considering counsel's advice as to whether the settlement is appropriate, all of which is designed to ensure that the protected party's interests are protected. That means that a case is not finalised until the approval hearing and any purported settlement can be undone until that point. Moreover, Limitation (see Chapter 19) does not start to run until the claimant achieves his majority or capacity to bring a claim.

The need to identify whether a party has capacity can therefore have real significance from a practitioner's perspective. It cannot simply be determined by reference to the claimant's age or appearance, a condition or an aspect of his behaviour which might lead others to make unjustified assumptions about his capacity, and it has to be more likely than not that he lacks capacity before steps can be taken to interfere with his making of decisions about the litigation. A psychiatric report is normally a suitable investigation at that stage.

It is also worth noting that in selecting a litigation friend, one should be careful to avoid a conflict of interest. In the case of the family involved in a road traffic accident, appointing the driver of the vehicle as the litigation friend for the children in the back seat might cause problems if it is alleged that the driver was partly, or wholly, at fault for the accident. Fortunately, one can always replace a litigation friend, even in the face of the court, as, for instance, in the circumstances where mother is the appointed litigation friend, but father brings the child to the approval hearing because mother is at work. One simply has to file a new Certificate of Suitability of Litigation Friend.

Finally, it is worth noting that in some cases there will be several claimants who will engage in group litigation, all of them suing the same defendant for the same tort. There are specific rules which apply to Group Litigation, set out in CPR19, but they fall outside this volume.

Defendants and Insurers

Similarly, one can have more than one defendant, either because there is a dispute between them as to who was to blame (e.g. the passenger in vehicle 1 sues both the driver of vehicle 1 and the driver of vehicle 2), or because they can each be said to blame (e.g. the driver of vehicle 1, hit by vehicle 2 and then again when vehicle 3 collides with vehicle 2 and causes a second impact). In some cases (see Chapter 5) a claimant can sue a number of defendants alleging that they have each caused or contributed to his injuries. For reasons which are discussed there, whilst there is no legal limit on the number of defendants, there are practical reasons why such cases are rare.

There are also cases where there are various different types of defendant. There might be a claim against an initial individual tortfeasor with a secondary claim against the hospital from which the injured claimant sought treatment. One of the most common cases, however, is that where the insurer (normally the motor insurer) is a party to the proceedings, either alongside the individual tortfeasor or in its own right. Those cases are discussed in chapter 6. Again, the rules governing the parties to litigation, to include adding and substituting parties, are set out in CPR19.

It is also worth noting that a defendant might have his own claim too. Sometimes, both sides bring their own claims simultaneously and the court has to bring the two actions together and resolve them consistently. It can be pure chance as to who is the claimant and who is the defendant with the counterclaim – one often sees the situation where the relatively modestly injured party is ready to start first, whilst the severely injured defendant needs more time to prepare his claim.

The Lawyers

As a general rule, the parties to litigation will engage a lawyer, but there are a number of reasons why they might choose to represent themselves (there is currently a move to replace the traditional terminology of 'Litigant In Person' with 'Self-Represented Party'). Successive governments have restricted, reduced and/or withdrawn funding for certain types of litigation and have limited the amount that a successful party might recover in respect of their own costs. They might not be able to afford a lawyer. They may not like what they have been told.

Equally, there are good reasons to utilise the services of a lawyer. They know the system and they understand what is required by the court. Rightly or wrongly, they are afforded respect by the opposition and the court. They have the time, understanding and experience to deal with matters efficiently and, critically, they should have a degree of detachment from the litigation which allows them to provide independent advice. The experienced lawyer should be able to provide a clear view of the potential endpoints of litigation, to allow the litigant to make the decisions to get the best outcome.

Solicitors' firms range in size from individuals to several hundred employees. Some firms specialise solely in personal injury law, whilst others have several different departments, offering specialist advice on a whole range of legal issues. Some of the workforce will be qualified solicitors, some might be qualified legal executives. There may be trainee solicitors, newly qualified solicitors, paralegals (often referred to as litigation executives) and the like. As a general rule, the less qualified or less experienced (neither of which means that they are necessarily less competent) fee earners will be supervised by the partners (who can charge more for their time). There will be other support staff working within the firm. The idea is that any given piece of work is done by the relevant person with the appropriate level of experience.

The solicitors (a general term at this stage, taking in all of the various fee earners and support staff at a firm) will undertake most, if not all, of the day to day running of a case. They are the first point of contact for the client, they write to the other side, they deal with the court, they arrange medical appointments, they take witness statements, they negotiate with the other side in correspondence or over the phone, and they undertake day to day, and, in certain circumstances, more complex advocacy. They are an integral part of the running of a claim, and often find themselves in the invidious position of trying to secure funding for expert evidence and court fees to allow the claimant to pursue his claim.

By contract, the barrister is normally self-employed, working for several different firms of solicitors. Whilst some decide to accept direct instructions, the traditional approach is that instructions have to come through a solicitor instructed by the client. The barrister's role was originally limited to drafting the relevant court documents, advising, whether in writing or in conference, as to the merits of the case and the steps to be taken to take the matter forward, and the courtroom advocacy of applications and trial. That has been expanded over the years with site visits, reviews of correspondence, assessing the strength of evidence and the like. Whilst many barristers are 'spare mouths', delivering a client's case with efficiency and eloquence to the court, many are 'spare brains', answering the questions to which the solicitors did not know the answer, providing a review and overview of the litigation, both to date and going forward, and providing an independent opinion on which the client might rely.

Neither solicitors nor barristers make the client's decisions for them – they simply advise. Whether the client himself understands that advice, or is prepared to listen to it, is an integral part of the challenge facing a lawyer when he is involved in the conduct of litigation.

CHAPTER THREE
AN OVERVIEW OF THE
LITIGATION PROCESS

The reality is that the vast majority of claims intimated do not reach a trial, either being compromised or withdrawn. Importantly, settlement can occur at, literally, any time. Some motor insurers make modest 'pre-medical' offers to buy off the potential for a claim, irrespective of whether the claimant has suffered injury, whilst some cases settle partway through the trial (or even pending appeal). This chapter deals briefly with what would happen when a case does not settle, but nevertheless runs smoothly through to trial as, surely, some must.

It is worth noting that there are a number of Protocols now in force under the Civil Procedure Rules 1998, each of which governs the appropriate pre-action conduct in a given type of case. Three of those Protocols are potentially relevant to this book: The Pre-Action Protocol for Personal Injury Claims, the Pre-Action Protocol for Disease and Illness Claims and the Pre-Action Protocol for Resolution of Clinical Disputes. The relevance of each is relatively straight-forward and the reader can consider them in his own time.

The Accident

This presupposes that this is a claim arising from a specific event rather than a course of conduct. The date of the accident is important because that is normally the starting point in time for the purposes of limitation (see Chapter 19).

Reporting the Accident

Depending on the circumstances of the accident, the first report will either be to a medical professional (most likely an A&E department) or to an employer or occupier of premises (who might want to record accidents in an accident book). When the first reporting of an accident is by way of notification of a claim, one has to question the extent to which one is actually injured.

The reporting of an accident can be critical. A defendant will often want to confirm that the contemporaneous medical records support the claimant's version of events. The records are not infallible. The writer once succeeded in a claim where the claimant said she'd fallen in a pothole, the paramedic record said that she'd fallen over a low wall after 7 or 8 pints, the A&E triage note said she'd fallen down a step in the garden, the orthopaedic note suggested she'd fallen on the back steps and the subsequent doctor's note said (accurately) that she could not give a clear explanation of how she came to be injured[1]. Fortunately the claimant had the independent witness who confirmed that she'd helped the claimant to her feet, believing that she'd sprained her ankle, only to discover that she'd also broken her wrist.

On the other hand, the claimant who averred that he'd fallen in the gulley running down the middle of the back alley behind his house struggled to elicit sympathy when the notes said that he'd 'fallen down back step', the court rejecting his suggestion that 'that's what everyone down our way calls it, at least in our house' in favour of the accident occurring on one of the dozen or so steps on the path running from his back door down to his back gate.

Notifying the claim

Normally by this point the claimant has appointed solicitors or has contacted an accident management company, although there is no reason why he cannot take this step himself.

Historically there would be a letter of claim, identifying the basis of the proposed claim, and in recent years clear guidance has been provided as to the contents of a letter of claim, but the majority of claims are now notified through the Claims Portal (www.claimsportal.org) with the claimant (or his representatives) completing an on-line form, certifying the truth of its contents. Unfortunately, those forms are all too often filled in inaccurately, with inconsistencies being picked up by defendants at a later date, even though the errors should have been obvious and should have been corrected. There is no good reason why a

---

1 Perhaps because aspects of the paramedic notes were accurate.

CHAPTER THREE – AN OVERVIEW OF THE LITIGATION PROCESS • 19

claimant should authorise the filing of a form stating that the weather was clear and sunny when the accident occurred at 11.30pm.

In response to the notification of the claim, the defendant (or more normally the insurer) can either admit or deny the claim, putting its own version of events on record and, if there is a dispute on the question of liability (or even if the defendant fails to respond in good time), the matter falls out of the Portal and proceeds by correspondence. The purpose of the Portal is to standardise the way in which claims are notified to defendants and record the relevant details centrally. Not all claims are intimated via the Portal (e.g. Clinical Negligence claims which have their own Protocol), but the purpose of notification is clear: the claimant tells the defendant that they are considering making a claim, which triggers, in turn, a need for a response.

Response

Upon receipt of a claim, a potential defendant can either admit liability, make a partial admission (e.g. an admission of primary liability but asserting contributory negligence), deny the claim (putting forward its own version of events and, depending on the applicable Protocol, sending relevant documentation to the claimant) or do nothing. Doing nothing can often lead to an application to compel the defendant to comply with the requirements of the relevant Protocol, and will normally cause the case to fall out of the Portal.

The purpose of notification and response is to allow the respective sides to draw up the relevant battle lines. They are not formalised at this stage – that is the purpose of Statements of Case (see below) and what is said at this stage in the correspondence is often a far cry from the case to be advanced at trial, but the majority of disputes are capable of settlement and this is the ideal opportunity for the parties to take stock.

Expert evidence

Obtaining suitable expert evidence is a topic for an entire book[2], but a claim for personal injury requires a claimant to prove that he has

---
2 c.f. *On Experts: CPR35 for Lawyers and Experts*, Law Brief Publishing (2016)

suffered an injury as a result of the defendant's tort, the extent of that injury and the likely prognosis. Once again, the starting point is the relevant Protocol[3]. The rules presuppose that experts will set out the range of possible opinions and identify their position within that range, owing their duty to the court rather than to the party instructing them. In simple claims, there is normally only one expert, and such is the nature of low level litigation that control over the identity of that expert is likely to vest in the claimant, who is unlikely to instruct an unsympathetic expert. In more complex claims, both sides might obtain expert evidence, often before litigation is formally commenced.

Supporting documentation

The claimant will need to prove his claim. As to proving the accident and liability, the documentation created by his reporting the accident and notifying the accident will become crucial, as will the documents which predate his accident, but which pertain to the circumstances giving rise to the accident (e.g. risk assessments, method statements, training records, inspection records) which tend to be held by the defendant and which should be disclosed as part of the Response phase, or to the claimant's pre-accident position (e.g. pay slips, medical records and the like) which tend to be held by the claimant. Again, these might reasonably be sent to the other side at an early stage if they are available, although often they are not.

If documents are not disclosed in accordance with the relevant Protocol, a party may make an application to the court for pre-action disclosure under CPR31.16. This requires an application notice with a witness statement and a fee is payable, but is not the same as formal proceedings between the two parties. The test is that both the applicant and the respondent is likely to be a party to subsequent proceedings, that if proceedings were started the respondent's duty under standard disclosure (see below) would extend to the documents sought and that disclosure before proceedings is desirable to dispose fairly of the anticipated proceedings, assist the dispute to be resolved without proceedings or to save costs. In other words, an applicant (normally the claimant)

---

3 And there are separate Protocols for road traffic accidents on the one hand and employers' and public liability claims on the other.

can ask to see a document which might help or hinder his case, either to assist him in formulating his claim, or to dissuade him from bringing it in the first place.

Negotiations

It is worth considering negotiations at this stage of the chronology, as this is the first time that the claimant is likely to be able to value his likely claim. He will have a medical report with, hopefully, some reasonable guidance as to what the future might hold and he will have started to formulate his claim for financial losses. Equally, the defendant will now be pushing for details of the likely claim so that they can consider whether this is one where a commercial view needs to be taken. Negotiations can (and should) continue throughout the course of a case, and the majority of claims can be resolved either before litigation or, in any event, before trial.

Whilst there are different mechanisms for making offers and negotiations can relate to anything from the most trivial issue right through to the settlement of the entire claim, there are two particularly significant points to bear in mind. Firstly, the majority of negotiations will be conducted on a 'Without Prejudice' basis. That means that, once the parties have identified the correspondence as being 'Without Prejudice (Save as to Costs[4])', the communication in question (and the communications flowing from that) cannot be relied upon in court until the issue of costs arises. In other words, if a defendant offers a claimant £5,000 on a without prejudice basis, the claimant cannot say to the judge: "Look judge, they've already offered me £5,000, so it must be worth more than that." On the other hand, if the offer is properly put (i.e. in accordance with CPR36 which deals with the making of offers and the effects of offers), the defendant can, at the end of the case, when the question of costs comes to be determined, say: "Look judge, we offered him £5,000 6 months ago, you've given him £4,500. The last 6 months have been a complete waste of time and the claimant should be penalised."

---

4 And this latter part of the phrase is often excluded, which, in turn, means that letter writers sometimes forget the true reason behind writing the phrase.

CPR36 has been one of the most changed of rules since 1999, although the gist of it has remained fairly constant. If a claimant makes an offer and then beats it at trial, he is entitled to various bonuses unless the court orders otherwise. Those bonuses may be additional damages, interest on his damages at a punitive rate, his costs on a more generous basis and interest on those costs. If, on the other hand, the defendant makes an offer and the claimant does not beat it at trial, the claimant only gets his costs from the defendant up to the point of the offer[5] and pays both his own costs and the costs of the defendant from that point. Given that a trial involves significant cost, that can wipe out much, if not all, of the damages.

That leads to the second critical point about negotiation, which is that any settlement has to deal with the issue of costs. If the settlement is silent as to costs, there is no order for costs between the parties. That means that negotiations will either commence with the claimant saying: "Any settlement will, of course, be conditional upon you paying our costs" or will include an express term of any given offer to the effect that "we will accept £x together with our costs".

Issue of Proceedings

There are a number of reasons why claimants choose to issue proceedings. There might be frustration with the defendant's lack of progress with the claim. There might be a realisation that the respective valuations require resolution by a judge. Sometimes a case is not yet ready, but an interim payment is required, so proceedings have to be issued.

Historically, to issue proceedings, a plaintiff would issue a writ, but the modern terminology requires a claimant to issue a Claim Form[6]. That means that he has to complete the relevant form, identifying who he wants to sue (to include their address), set out the brief details of the claim (which normally include the relevant date of the incident) and certify the contents as true. Three copies of that document are prepared (assuming only one defendant) and are sent (or taken) to court, along

---

5 Actually 21 days after the offer, because that it is standard period allowed for acceptance.

6 CPR16.2

with a fee which depends on the sum of money being claimed. The court stamps those documents and records on their face the date on which the claim was issued. The case is assigned a unique case number, and the issued Claim Form is either served directly upon the named defendant by the court, or returned to the claimant's solicitor for service in due course.

The relevance of the date of issue goes to the question of Limitation (see Chapter 12). The claimant is supposed to bring his claim within 3 years of the accident. Traditionally, that meant that the Claim Form had to be issued, such that a junior fee earner could be sent to the local county court with a cheque and the various documents and would have to wait until a member of the court office staff stamped the Claim Form and returned it. Claim Forms are now issued centrally in the County Court Money Claims Centre, nominally based in Northampton, but also operating in Salford, so the relevant date for deciding whether the claimant has issued in time is the date on which the papers are delivered to the court, not the date, often some days later, when they make their way through an administrative backlog and are given a case number.

The Particulars of Claim[7]

The Particulars of Claim is a formal document, signed with a Statement of Truth, setting out the legal basis of the claimant's claim. It can be very simple, or several pages long depending on the facts, although it should be as straight-forward as possible:

The parties should be identified. Traditionally, certain formal phrases appear: "1. At all material times, the defendant was the driver of a Ford Focus, registration ABC1, and the claimant was the front seat passenger therein." This goes to establish the nature of the duty of care (see Chapter 5).

The factual events leading up to the claimant being injured should be set out: "2. On 1 April 2016 the defendant was driving along High Street, Sometown, when he lost control of the vehicle and collided with a tree."

---

7   CPR16.4

The allegations of breach of duty should be set out: "3. The defendant was negligent in that he: (a) lost control of the vehicle and (b) collided with a tree."

Brief particulars of the injury should be included, together with the claimant's date of birth and details of any medical evidence being served with the Particulars of Claim: "4. The claimant, who was born on 1 January 1997, suffered a displaced fracture of his nose which was reset in A&E, his symptoms resolving by some 6 weeks post-accident. Further details of the claimant's injuries are set out in the report of Dr Smith, dated 1 June 2016, served herewith)." Any other financial losses can be set out at this stage.

Any claim for interest on damages should be included on the face of the Particulars of Claim. Further details of what should be included appear in CPR16.4 and PD16.

Service[8]

Once the claimant has issued his Claim Form, he needs to bring it to the attention of the defendant by serving a copy in a manner prescribed by the rules.

If the claimant is ready for proceedings to be served on a defendant and has included all relevant documents with the Claim Form when it is sent to court, they can be sent by post, straight away, to the defendant. Equally, the claimant might not be ready to serve all the documentation and get the case moving. He might not have a medical report yet. He might not have the Particulars of Claim drafted. There are a number of reasons why there might be a delay in serving the documents and the rules permit him 4 months in which to effect service on the defendant.

The rules on service are set out in CPR7.5 and are strict. After all, if you haven't started proceedings properly, you can't rely on the rules of court which apply to properly commenced proceedings. Service can be effected either in person, by post, or, in certain circumstances, by elec-

---

8 CPR7.5

tronic or other means. Of course, tracking down a man known only as 'John' on an industrial estate in Dudley, who says that he knows the defendant and can get the papers to him, does not, whatever one might think, constitute effective service.

Acknowledgement of Service[9]

Once the defendant has received the formal court papers he needs to file the appropriate form (which is included with the papers served), informing the court that he has received the papers and setting out what he intends to do with the claim – either admitting it, contesting it, or disputing the jurisdiction of the court (which includes arguments about the validity of service – see CPR11).

If the defendant fails to file an Acknowledgement of Service within 14 days, the claimant can ask the court to enter judgment in default of acknowledgment. This allows the claimant to progress his claim fairly swiftly if a defendant is ignoring the issue and hoping that it will go away, but equally, the court might set aside that judgment in due course if it transpires that the defendant has a defence with a real prospect of success, assuming, of course, that the defendant makes that application within a reasonable time period.

Defence[10]

The defendant should, either with the Acknowledgement of Service or within 14 days of it, serve a Defence, setting out which parts of the Particulars of Claim are admitted, which are denied (and the reasons for that denial) and which can neither be admitted nor denied. Again, the rules set out what is and isn't appropriate on the face of a Defence: "The defendant denies the version of events in paragraph 2 of the Particulars of Claim and avers that the tree fell into the road directly in front of him, giving him no opportunity to avoid an accident, even though he was only travelling at 10mph at that point in time." would do the job.

---

9   CPR10

10 CPR16.5

Unfortunately, one often sees hyperbole at this point. "The defendant denies in the strongest possible terms that…" is wholly unnecessary when the argument will have to be decided on the balance of probability.

The Defence should also set out the defendant's position in respect of the various aspects of the claimant's claim and any counterclaim which the defendant might want to bring.

Reply[11]

The claimant might feel that the Defence (or Counterclaim) requires a response and can file a Reply setting out his position vis-à-vis the Defence. Technically, a defendant can respond to the Reply by way of a Rejoinder, but will require the permission of the court to take that step. In 22 years, the writer has drafted two Rejoinders and been the recipient of a third.

Directions

Once the parties have set out their respective positions in these formal documents, the court gives directions about how the case is to proceed to trial. Directions questionnaires are sent out to the parties, which have to be completed and sent back to the court by a specified date, to include their proposals for the timetabling of the case. The court will then either set out a timetable without a hearing or, if the case warrants it and/or there are contested issues, list a hearing where the parties attend. In some cases, only partial directions are given and the case is listed for another hearing so that the court can make an informed decision about what might happen next. These hearings are known as Case Management Conferences.

Tracking

A case is normally allocated to a track. The Small Claims Track is for claims of limited value, where the costs which might be recovered by a claimant are very modest indeed. Before 1996 the limit was £1,000, but

---

11 CPR15.8

in 1996 the limit for non-personal injury claims was increased to £3,000, since when it has risen to £5,000 and £10,000. The limit for personal injury claims remained at £1,000, despite inflation, until 2017 when the government proposed to increase the limit to £2,000 for normal personal injury claims and introduced a new tariff for whiplash injuries. The important point about the Small Claims Track is that the costs recoverable are so limited that they represent little more than one or two hours of a lawyer's time. Litigants either have to represent themselves, or instruct a lawyer knowing that the cost will outweigh the potential benefits.

The Fast Track is appropriate for claims worth up to £25,000 and which can be dealt with in a day. The rules now provide for fixed tariffs for the costs recoverable in the Fast Track. Whilst these are more generous than the costs in the Small Claims Track, they are unlikely to reflect the amount of work required to take a case to trial. Corners inevitably get cut, with cheaper fee earners required to process such claims.

The Multi Track is appropriate for larger value claims, claims with more complexity to them, or claims which will last more than a day. Whilst the parties can charge hourly rates for their work on such claims, they are normally the subject of budgeting, with the court identifying at a relatively early stage what can be spent on any given phase of the proceedings. Both sides exchange budgets, normally in spreadsheet form, with the court assessing the hours likely to be needed and the costs which might be incurred. This can either take place at the Case Management Conference (rendering it a Costs and Case Management Conference) or at a separate hearing if necessary.

Disclosure and Inspection

This is the formal process of exchanging relevant documents and ensuring that both sides have complied with their obligations in this regard. Disclosure is made by listing documents, or classes of documents, on a formal list, divided into three categories: documents to be relied upon, documents which are privileged, and documents which are not (or no longer) in the party's possession. The other party can then request inspection of the documents in the first category. These two distinct phases are often elided in the minds of lawyer and litigants, who forget that one can 'disclose' a document by stating either that it is privileged or that it is no longer in their possession.

If a party does not disclose a document, he cannot rely upon it at trial, without the permission of the court. That can lead to the difficult situation where a party arrives at court wanting to rely upon a critical document. The court might not allow him to rely upon it at all, or may order that the case be adjourned to allow the other side to consider the document and to investigate either its veracity or whether it can be countered, or simply to take stock as to the effects of that document on the case.

Witness Statements

Witness statements are exchanged, normally a short time after Inspection. Such a document should be drafted in the witness's own words (normally observed in the breach) and should be capable of supporting each and every aspect of the party's case at trial. One should never assume that the judge will allow a witness to give new evidence at trial if it is not already addressed in the witness statement.

Medical evidence

The directions will include permission for one or both parties to rely upon medical evidence and allow the parties to ask questions of the experts pursuant to CPR35. Evidence at trial is normally restricted to the written reports unless there is a conflict of evidence which requires the experts to attend to be cross-examined.

Schedules and Counter-Schedules

The parties set out their respective positions about the various heads of loss being sought in formal documents which form the battle lines for both negotiations and trial.

Trial

All of the various steps set out above are aimed at getting the case to a trial and asking a judge to decide the unresolved issues between the parties. Of course, the vast majority of cases do not get that far, not least because the reasonable litigant will have regard to the rule of three for claimants and the rule of three for defendants.

A personal injury trial, as with most civil trials, is heard by a judge. That might be a district judge (Sir/Ma'am), a circuit judge (Your Honour), or even a high court judge (M'Lord/M'Lady)[12]. They might hold that role part-time. Deputy district judges and Recorders[13] are a mainstay of the judiciary, either being practitioners who sit as judges for a set number of days per year, or retired full-time judges who keep their hand in. Deputy high court judges are either highly experienced practitioners or highly experienced circuit judges who are given a temporary promotion to allow them to hear the case.

One of the parties, normally the claimant, has to provide the court with an agreed trial bundle in advance of the trial. This is to allow the court to read the papers and identify the core issues in order to conduct the trial efficiently. The bundle should be paginated with the relevant statements of case, schedules, counter-schedules, court orders, lay witness statements, medical evidence and documents, although many suffer from including pages and pages which will never trouble the court. An understanding of what the court will need to make its decision is therefore a good starting point. One can always identify the core documents in one bundle and other, potentially useful but more probably irrelevant, ones in a secondary bundle, available to all for reference. In certain cases, the solicitor will bring the full file to court.

The difficulty is often that a case will run for so long that it is hard to achieve the necessary distillation of the issues and/or the documentation before trial. The important point is this: a party should prepare a case

---

12 Having seen litigants address judges as everything from Duck to Your Highness Sir, it is worth letting them know the correct form of address beforehand.

13 The title of a deputy circuit judge, not to be confused with the Honorary Recorder of (e.g.) Manchester – the top ranking full-time Criminal Circuit Judge in the city.

on the basis that it will get to trial and that his actions will be assessed by the court. His disclosure should be properly considered. His witness statement should balance the need to be thorough with the need to get his point across, and should concentrate on the real issues in the case. A little thought about what is or isn't important makes a statement far more compelling when it is read by the judge, and if it's true, that will become clear. The real nub of personal injury litigation is to identify the appropriate end point of the process and to work out how to get there, rather than just advancing, one step at a time, across a minefield, towards the enemy's machine gun posts.

The trial itself normally falls into 4 sections:

(a) The opening: The claimant brings the case and has to prove it. He (or his advocate) starts proceedings by explaining the issues in the case to the court. Some of that is normally reduced to writing, either by way of a case summary (which should be neutral and informative) or a skeleton argument (which can be more partisan), served in advance of trial so that the judge might read ahead. The oral opening will normally take in housekeeping issues, evidential points which might arise, the relevant documents and/or sections of the trial bundle and the likely running order of witnesses. The task is to get the court onside at the outset.

(b) The evidence: The claimant normally calls his evidence in the case before the defendant does, although there are occasions where the limited availability of a witness means that he gives his evidence out of order. One would hope that the court can deal with the confusion that this might cause. In the normal course of events, witnesses sit in court throughout the proceedings, listening to the evidence being given before them. This can be a double-edged sword, as the later witnesses can be influenced, often incorrectly, by those giving evidence ahead of them.

Each witness, in giving evidence, goes through the same process. He enters the witness box, takes an oath or affirms depending

CHAPTER THREE – AN OVERVIEW OF THE LITIGATION PROCESS • 31

on his preference, and confirms his name, his address and the truth of his witness statement. If necessary, he can (and should) correct anything in his statement before confirming its contents. If a witness gets his name or address wrong, it normally bodes ill.

The witness statement normally stands as the evidence in chief, just as if it were read out. The written statement forms part of the court record. There might be some supplementary questions in chief, but normally one then proceeds straight to cross-examination where the other side puts its case to the witness and attempts to discredit him. The witness can be re-examined by his own advocate in respect of anything raised in cross-examination, and the judge might well ask questions of his own. Once the evidence has been completed, the witness is normally 'released' so that he can leave court, although he can still be recalled if the judge directs.

(c) Submissions: At the end of the defendant's evidence, the defendant (by his advocate) normally makes the first submission, explaining to the court why it should find in his favour. The claimant then makes his submissions. If the defendant chooses not to call any evidence, the claimant normally makes submissions before the defendant.

(d) Judgment: The judge might take some time to plan his judgment, or deliver it straight away. It should set out the background to the dispute, the respective positions, the evidence, the judge's findings of fact and the conclusions drawn as to the questions of liability, causation and quantum. The judgment should be sufficient for the parties to understand it and to know the basis on which the court reached its decision. If there are glaring omissions, a party who might want to appeal on that basis should identify the potential default to the judge. The judgment phase normally concludes with arguments about costs and an order being drawn which will be formalised and which will represent a permanent reminder of the decision made.

Hopefully, by identifying the desired end-point, a litigant can better judge how each step along the way can be taken to maximise the chance of success.

CHAPTER FOUR
THE LEGAL MATRIX AND
THE LAW OF TORT

The law of tort (or torts) is a core subject within a Law degree. This book is not designed to take the place of that level of study, but it is worth remembering that, in order to secure compensation, a claimant needs to prove first that the defendant owed him a duty of care; second, that the defendant breached that duty of care; third that the defendant's breach of duty caused his, the claimant's, injury; and fourth that he, the claimant, has suffered loss as a result.

Duty of Care

The concept and formulation of a duty of care forms much of one's academic study of tort. In the real world, the question is normally relatively straight-forward. If you are a motorist, you normally owe a duty of care to other road users, unless they are involved in a joint enterprise with you, the tortfeasor, to drive in a dangerous manner. If you are injured as a result of your own wrongdoing, you are unlikely to be owed a duty of care, unless the law specifically provides for one. If you are an employer, you owe a duty of care to your employee. Whilst academia inevitably strays towards the edges of what is or might be a tort, the real world tends to be much simpler. There will, of course, be occasional cases which fall close to the line, particularly where, for instance, there is a claim for psychiatric, rather than physical, injury.

Breach of Duty

Similarly, the question of breach tends to be a fact-sensitive issue, rather than a legal one. The legal framework will decide whether the duty is absolute, so that any technical breach is enough; one where the obligation on the defendant is to show that it took all reasonably practicable steps to avoid the accident; or whether it is a straight-forward matter of whether the defendant failed to take reasonable care in all the circumstances. The first question tends to be: "What actually happened?" followed by "Why did that happen?" and once those questions are answered (on the balance of probability), that normally suffices to determine whether there has been a breach of duty. Sometimes, the question of breach of duty is an integral part of whether loss has been caused and vice versa. This arises particularly in cases where the claimant claims to have sustained noise-induced hearing loss, where the question of whether the claimant's loss has been caused by a breach of duty depends to some extent on whether the claimant can prove that he has suffered a loss of the type caused by a breach of duty.

Causation

The question of causation is probably one of the most difficult issues in personal injury law, particularly when a claimant's condition has more than one potential cause. In some cases, the issue is easy: If I fall in a hole and break my wrist, the breach of duty in allowing that hole to come about and remain in place has caused, both in law and in fact, my injury. The answer might be different if, for instance, I had seen the hole and was deliberately walking alongside it, only to step, unthinkingly, to one side because of an oncoming cyclist on the pavement. His negligent riding has undoubtedly caused my accident, but has the digging of the hole? And to what extent am I responsible too?

That last point raises the question of contributory negligence. In any case where the claimant himself might have contributed to the accident or to his injury then that responsibility falls to be taken 'off the top' before considering the respective responsibility of the potential tortfeasors.

Most of the law as to causation, however, depends on whether the injury suffered by the claimant is a "divisible" (or cumulative) condition where each defendant is liable for his own contribution to the claimant's injury or an indivisible injury where the question is one of whether the defendant materially contributed to the claimant's injury, in which case each such defendant is potentially "jointly and severally" liable for the claimant's loss.

An example of a divisible condition is noise induced hearing loss where a claimant might have been exposed to excessive noise in a series of jobs, each causing some damage to his hearing. In those circumstances, one would value the entire claim, apportion the exposure between the defendants (normally on a time basis, but also allowing for different levels of exposure, different working conditions and, potentially, non-negligent exposure) with each defendant contributing their share, no matter how small. This means that in circumstances where an employer is no longer in existence and/or no insurance can be found the claimant will inevitably have to sacrifice that proportion of his damages.

On the other hand, in the case of an indivisible condition (e.g. cancer), where the claimant either has it, or does not, the fact that one of the potential defendants cannot be sued (for similar reasons to those set out above) does not prevent the claimant pursuing the claim against any one remaining defendant for the totality of his damages.

This is by necessity a fairly simplistic approach to the question of causation, but one which will allow the reader a sensible starting point.

Loss

Ultimately, it is for the claimant to prove that he has suffered loss as a result of the defendant's breach of duty. This book is about personal injury law and the question will be, in the first instance, what did the breach of duty cause the claimant to suffer? Has he suffered a new injury that, but for the breach of duty, he would never have suffered? Has he an underlying condition (whether previously symptomatic or not) which has been aggravated, exacerbated, accelerated, or otherwise affected by the breach of duty? What other losses has the claimant incurred as a result?

Those questions will be analysed in a later chapter. In some cases, the law restricts the type of loss which is recoverable. Pure economic loss is the most talked about concept at undergraduate level although in the context of personal injury law the restrictions on recovering damages for psychiatric injury are perhaps more relevant. Again, those are issues which fall outside the scope of this work.

Conclusion

For these purposes it is imperative that the reader understands that each of the above hoops must be jumped through successfully by the claimant, who bears the burden of proof in the normal run of events, failing which his claim will fail. From a claimant's perspective, one needs to address each of these issues in turn at the start of the case to see whether he is going to run into trouble. It is all very well getting excited about a breach of duty if in fact it was not a causative breach. A defendant may be in breach of duty if he places a builder's skip on the highway without lights, warning cones, suitable fluorescent markings, and without an appropriate permit, but if the claimant simply drives into it in daylight hours when it takes up the exact same space as a parked car might, he cannot complain: the accident was his fault.

PART TWO

ROAD TRAFFIC ACCIDENTS

CHAPTER FIVE
INSURANCE AND THE MIB

Given that the purpose of bringing a claim for personal injuries is to recover damages, the question of whether a defendant can satisfy a judgment is clearly of significant import. After all, a car can be bought cheaply, or even stolen, and then driven in such a way as to cause potentially very serious injuries.

In the normal course of events, if a defendant collides with a claimant and causes him injury and loss, the claimant sues the defendant directly, claiming damages. Clearly, the defendant might be incredibly rich and might be able to pay the claimant's damages out of his own pocket, but the majority of people rely on their insurance company to satisfy any judgment.

Section 143 of the Road Traffic Act 1988 requires the user of a motor vehicle to hold an insurance policy in respect of third party risks (i.e. any claim which might be made against the driver by another person) and makes it an offence not to hold such a policy or to allow such a vehicle to be driven without a relevant policy.

Despite the fact that the law requires anybody driving a car to hold a policy of insurance, there are at least 4 different scenarios which arise in practice, and it is worth considering them here.

Scenario 1 – Indemnified drivers

The normal scenario, then, is that the negligent driver (the 'insured') holds an insurance policy with the insurer, and the insurer is contractually bound to (and agrees to) indemnify the tortfeasor for the effects of his actions.

Traditionally, the claimant would bring an action against the insured as the only defendant, but, either before or within 7 days of commencing proceedings, he would give notice to the relevant insurer under section 152 of the Road Traffic Act 1988, which, in turn, activates the provisions of section 151.

Section 151 requires the insurer to satisfy any judgment which the claimant might obtain against the insured. The insurance policy allows the insurer to take such steps as are necessary to protect its position (and that of the insured) and the insurer stands in the insured's shoes for the purposes of the litigation. That can cause some difficulties where, for instance, an insured has a counterclaim, but those issues normally fall to be decided between the insurer and the insured, rather than in the litigation. The important point is that the requirements of section 151 and 152 are such that once there is a relevant policy in place, the claimant is entitled to have his judgment paid by that insurer, irrespective of any issues which arise between the tortfeasor and his insurance company (see Scenario 2 below).

As an alternative, if the insurer has confirmed indemnity to the insured, the claimant can actually name the insurer as the defendant to the action, pursuant to the European Communities (Rights Against Insurers) Regulations 2002. Rather than pleading that the defendant negligently drove into collision with the claimant's vehicle, the claimant avers that the insurer granted a policy to the insured, who, in turn, drove into the claimant's vehicle. That way, the claimant can bring an action directly to the attention of the insurance company, minimising delays.

Which method is correct? The short answer is that there are merits to each. Naming the tortfeasor as the defendant makes far more sense if there is going to be a dispute on liability or a counterclaim, because of the artificial nature of a pleading under the Regulations, but if the action is a straight-forward one, liability is admitted and the only issue is the amount of the damages, is there any real need to include the insured at all?

One circumstance where the Regulations are particularly useful is where the precise identity of the driver is for some reason unknown but whoever was driving would have been covered by the policy of insurance, in which circumstances the claimant can plead and prove that the insurer insured the vehicle and covered whichever person happened to be driving it at the time.

Another situation where the Regulations are potentially useful is where the claimant and the defendant are related to one another. Clearly that normally happens when the injured person is a passenger in the defendant's vehicle, although the writer was once involved in a difficult case where two brothers had collided on a blind bend outside the family farm. In these cases, the insurer often agrees to be joined to the proceedings, either in parallel to the tortfeasor or in substitution, because it allows both sides to be objective and realistic about the fact that the injured person and the person who caused the injury live together and may both have a vested interest in the outcome of the claim.

Importantly, if the case is to be brought under the Regulations and the insurer is not taking issue with that, only the insurer need be named as a defendant.

Scenario 2 – Non-indemnified drivers

In some circumstances, an insurer will decide that, whilst it is the relevant insurer vis-à-vis the accident and the claimant's claim, a problem with the contract of insurance means that it is not obliged to indemnify its insured. The claimant is still entitled to the judgment sum, and the insurer has to pay that sum, but the insurer can then ask its insured for repayment of those monies.

There are three common scenarios where indemnity is refused. The first is where the information given when the policy was taken out (or at least before the accident) was not, in fact, accurate, so that the requirement of utmost good faith is broken. Examples are where the insured has moved address, works part-time in a profession which is deemed to be of higher risk (e.g. doorman), has failed to declare previous convictions, or is 'fronting' the policy for an inexperienced driver, suggesting that the older (and therefore nominally lower risk) driver is the main driver when, in fact, the younger driver spends more time behind the wheel. Section 152(2) of the Road Traffic Act 1988 allows an insurer, faced with a claim, to seek a declaration that they are entitled to void the policy for non-disclosure of a material fact or by a misrepresentation. That application has to be obtained within 3 months of the commencement of proceedings. Ironically, the insurer normally ends up dealing with the matter as the Article 75 (or 'Domestic Regs') insurer in any event. They have certain additional protections in that role, but they are unlikely to escape entirely.

The second scenario is where the person driving the car at the material time is not, in fact, the insured. Where an insured has allowed an uninsured driver to use the vehicle, the policy still has to pay out, but the insurer can ask either or both of the uninsured driver and the insured driver who allowed him to drive, to refund the insurer's outlay, pursuant to section 151(8) of the Road Traffic Act 1988. There is an interesting question as to what happens when the injured party is also the insured person who allowed the uninsured person to drive in the first place.[1]

The third scenario is where, after the accident, the insurer can show that the insured has either not cooperated with the requirements of the policy or has been acting against the insurer's interests (e.g. by seeking to defraud the insurer by becoming involved in a fraudulent scheme). It is not proposed to discuss fraudulent claims in this book – it would require a complete volume – but such circumstances are increasingly common.

In any of the above circumstances, the insurer will need to be involved in the action, because it has a financial interest in the outcome, but the alleged tortfeasor will also have to be involved in their own right. They will be entitled to take part in the proceedings and should be kept abreast of what is happening. The effects is that there will have to be at least 2 defendants, with the tortfeasor potentially supporting the claimant on the question of whether the accident occurred or not, disputing liability for the accident, and siding with the insurer when it comes to issues of valuation. The court will ultimately have to decide whether the claimant falls to be compensated and whether the tortfeasor is entitled to the protection of his contracted indemnity.

---

1 *Churchill Insurance Company v Fitzgerald & Wilkinson and others* [2012] EWCA Civ 1166

Scenario 3 – Uninsured drivers

The third situation which one might see is where the negligent driver has not, in fact, bothered to obtain a policy of insurance at all, so that there is no relevant insurer. This, logically, puts the claimant in the difficult position of having to secure and enforce a judgment against a man of straw. Fortunately, since 1946, such claimants have had the benefit of the Motor Insurers' Bureau Uninsured Drivers Agreement. Whilst the Agreement itself has changed over the years, the basic principle has remained the same. The victim of an uninsured driver can bring an action against that driver and join the Motor Insurers' Bureau (a private company limited by guarantee) to the proceedings as a separate defendant. If the claimant obtains a judgment against the tortfeasor which goes unsatisfied because there is no relevant insurer, the MIB satisfies that judgment and any costs order. The MIB can act more proactively and will, if it can, secure an agreement from the tortfeasor which will allow the MIB to settle the matter and then pursue the tortfeasor if that is practicable.

There are clear parallels between Scenario 2 and Scenario 3. In each case, the tortfeasor is normally named as the first defendant whilst the insurer, or MIB as the case might be, is the second defendant. Proper notice has to be given to the second defendant before they are obliged to satisfy any judgment, there are hoops through which the claimant must jump and the second defendant normally has a right of recovery against the tortfeasor. The victim of negligence is protected in any event.

Scenario 4 – Unidentified drivers

The final scenario is one where there is an accident, but the negligent party cannot be identified, either because they did not stop at the scene, or because the information provided at the scene turns out to be false. In those circumstances, there is no tortfeasor against whom the claimant might bring a claim. The MIB, however, also operates the Untraced Drivers Agreement. This is an administrative, rather than litigated exercise. An application is made to the scheme, evidence can be obtained, and modest costs are allowed to allow the injured party some independent advice, but the premise is that the MIB makes an administrative decision on the evidence available and can make an award, either in terms of an apportionment of liability, or a global sum. Any challenge to that decision can be referred to an arbitrator under the scheme, and any appeal against that decision would have to be by way of judicial review.

The Untraced Drivers Agreement can, on certain facts, run alongside a litigated case. One example is the situation where two cars are travelling alongside each other, only for a third party to pull out from a side road, seeking to establish themselves in one or other lane, causing the driver in that lane to swerve into collision with the parallel driver. The third party vehicle then leaves the scene, leaving the remaining drivers to argue about who is to blame. That matter might be litigated, with the losing driver then having to make a claim to the MIB on the basis that his actions were caused in part by the negligence of an unidentified driver.

It is worth bearing in mind that if one can identify the vehicle, which is covered by a policy of insurance, but not the driver (perhaps because he gives a false name), there is the possibility of bringing an action against that unknown driver and the relevant insurer rather than going down the Untraced Driver route.[2]

Last resort

The MIB, under whichever incarnation, is only ever a port of last resort. If an insurer can be identified, that insurer has to pick up the bill before the MIB has to pay. The reason for this is that the MIB is, in effect, funded by the insurance industry. As a result, if an insured driver is even 1% to blame for the accident, that insurer pays the whole claim. The same applies whether the MIB involvement is under the Uninsured or Untraced Scheme. In effect, the law acknowledges that in a case of joint and several liability a claimant can recover against any defendant who materially contributed to his loss, and, in the case of the MIB, obliges the claimant to pursue the insured defendant rather than the Bureau.

---

2 *Cameron v Hussain et al.* [2017] EWCA Civ 366

To put that into context, the writer was once involved in a case where A was driving a campervan along a country road, at night, looking for a place to make a U turn. He saw a road to the right, checked his mirror, noted some lights some distance back and went to make a manoeuvre, only for B, who was actually very close behind him, to perform a successful overtaking manoeuvre. A, shocked, braked hard and came to a stop in the middle of the road, whereupon C collided with the back of the campervan. C and his passengers D and E were injured. B left the scene and, it transpired, had no insurance. A sued C on the basis that he had collided with the rear of his vehicle. C counterclaimed saying that A should not have stopped in the middle of the road, and that he had done so because he was surprised by B's overtaking manoeuvre, having been unaware of B when he should have been. B played no part in the proceedings and D and E awaited the outcome.

One possible finding would be that blame should be apportioned 20:50:30 between A, B and C. In those circumstances, A would sue C and accept a 20% reduction for contributory negligence, getting judgment for 80% of his claim against Claimant (because C would have to pick up any liability which might otherwise be apportioned to the MIB). C, however, would counterclaim and accept a 30% reduction for his share of contributory negligence, getting judgment for 70% of his claim against A (who, for these purposes, would have to pick up the MIB's share). D and E's claims would then fall to be compromised 40:60 against A and C respectively, so that one could have had 20%, 30%, 40%, 50%, 60%, 70% *and* 80% apportionments within the one case. Regrettably, history does not record the outcome.

CHAPTER SIX
THE LEGAL ISSUES

Duty of Care

The driver of a car potentially owes a duty of care to a number of different categories of individual. He clearly owes a duty of care to other road users, whether other drivers, passengers in other vehicles, passengers in his own vehicle, or pedestrians.

There are, however, some circumstances where no duty is owed: the passenger may be party, with the driver, to a criminal act: joyriding, having taken the car without the consent of the owner, or racing with another vehicle. Where there is an element of joint enterprise giving rise to the tortious behaviour of the defendant, the claimant, being party to that otherwise negligent act, cannot complain that he suffered injury as a result. Lawyers often refer to the Latin maxim *ex turpi causa non oritur actio* ("no action arises from a dishonourable cause"), often shortened to *ex turpi causa* or just *ex turpi*. The idea is that a claimant should not benefit from (or at least be compensated for) an unlawful act.

There are, of course, different levels of illegality. Much as a defendant might want to aver that a claimant whose car insurance expired at midnight was driving illegally at 1 o'clock and thus is not entitled to compensation when the defendant collides with him, the activity being undertaken is a lawful activity, albeit carried out in a manner contrary to the law. That does not give rise to a defence in law. Were that the case, the claimant travelling at 31 mph in a 30 zone would arguably be deprived of any damages should somebody pull out in front of him. The rule is aimed directly at those engaged in mischief from the off.

Whilst a duty of care is still owed by the driver to his passengers, that does not mean that the insurer is liable to satisfy any judgement where the claimant falls into one of the statutory exceptions, such as that provided by section 151(4) of the Road Traffic Act 1988 which excludes liability to a passenger who allows himself to be carried in or upon the vehicle and knew or had reason to believe that the vehicle had been stolen or unlawfully taken. Similar exclusions apply under the

Motor Insurers' Bureau Uninsured Drivers Agreement where there is no liability accruing to the passenger who knows, or who reasonably ought to have known that the driver was not insured. An example would be where the passenger knew the driver had not passed his test or had previously been disqualified.

Breach of Duty

The question of what is a breach of duty by a driver is normally a fairly clear-cut one. The criminal law recognises two levels of criminal driving: "careless" driving which falls "below the level of the reasonably competent driver" and "dangerous" driving which falls "*well* below the level of the reasonably competent driver", whilst in the civil law, the claimant need only show that the defendant's driving was "below" the standard. In other words, if the driver was careless or was driving without due care (and in particular if he has been convicted of an offence of careless or dangerous driving) then he is negligent and in breach of his duty. That breach can take a number of forms: The driver might have been travelling too quickly, might not have seen another road user in time or at all, might have moved onto the wrong side of the road, executed a turn when it was not safe to do so, or simply have lost control. In each such case he is likely to be in breach of duty, although whether that is causative depends on all the circumstances.

The important issue in cases such as this is that of "thinking time": the inevitable delay between a driver identifying a potential problem and being able to respond to it. Whilst the Highway Code traditionally suggests a thinking time of two-thirds of a second, there are a number of factors which can affect that. A more realistic timescale is between one and two seconds. The prevailing conditions can have an effect, particularly if the accident occurs at night. Older drivers tend to have slightly slower reaction times. In some cases, it can be difficult to detect the hazard itself: if a vehicle ahead moves in its lane, is that because it intends to change lanes or simply because the driver has drifted slightly from the original line? Is that pedestrian waiting to step out going to attempt to cross the road or will they simply step from the kerb and then stop to allow traffic to pass? It can be difficult to identify the intention of another road user.

Causation and Contributory Negligence

The question of what is causative will depend on the facts of the case. Importantly, as we've already seen, even a 1% contribution to the overall accident can be deemed to be causative.

One commonly seen question of causation, or more realistically contributory negligence, is the failure to wear a seatbelt. If the claimant suffers injury as a result of not wearing a seatbelt, and would otherwise have been uninjured, his damages will be reduced by 25% to reflect the causative potency of his failure to wear the seatbelt. If he would have been injured to some extent but not to the extent that he was in fact injured, that reduction is 15%. If he would have been injured to the same extent in any event there is no reduction because there is no causative effect of that negligence. The burden of proof when alleging contributory negligence falls on the defendant. In normal circumstances one might ask questions of the reporting medical expert as to the effects of wearing or not wearing a seatbelt, although in certain circumstances more specialist expert evidence will be required from a road safety engineer specialising in the effects of seatbelt use.

Another commonly seen circumstance is that of a vehicle colliding with a pedestrian as the latter crosses the road. While such cases invariably turn to some extent on the facts, as a general rule the motorist, having control of a fast-moving large lump of metal, will be held more to blame than the pedestrian because the causative potency of his negligence will outweigh the moral turpitude (blameworthiness) of the pedestrian. There are a number of cases supporting the basic contention that the pedestrian who negligently walks out in front of a car is 1/3 to blame[1] (assuming that negligence can be proven against the driver). The pedestrian who stands in the middle of the road, ignoring instructions to get themselves to a safe place, may still only be 40% to blame.[2]

---

1 e.g. *Lunt v Khelifa* [2002] EWCA Civ 801, *Smith v Chief Constable of Nottinghamshire Police* [2012] EWCA Civ 161

2 *Eagle v Chambers* [2003] EWCA Civ 1107

CHAPTER SEVEN
THE FACTUAL ISSUES

The question of what is and isn't negligent in the circumstances of a road traffic accident is invariably fact sensitive. That said, there are a relatively finite number of ways in which a road traffic accident is likely to occur. Whilst the list below is not a closed list it provides a good starting point.

The Rear End Shunt

The defendant collides with the rear of the claimant's vehicle, the claimant averring that the defendant was too close behind him, was driving too quickly and did not realise in time that he needed to bring his own vehicle to a halt. The defendant, by contrast, might suggest that the claimant had pulled out in front of him without indicating or had stopped for no reason or that his brake lights were not working. There is a current trend towards drivers seeking to explain their own negligence by blaming the claimant for stopping unnecessarily. In some cases that is correct and there is a deliberate attempt by the claimant to cause an accident, but the more likely scenario is that there is a good reason for the claimant to have slowed and the defendant has simply made a mistake. One often sees accidents arising from the negligent driving of a third party who, having caused the claimant to slow unexpectedly (at least as far as the defendant is concerned), then leaves the scene, potentially oblivious to what he has done. The defendant may well aver that he was not himself negligent but the reality is that, if he is 1% to blame, the absence of the third party will not help him. The critical issues in such a case tend to come down to distance, speed, time and observation. Defendants often run cases along the lines that the driving of the unknown third party was consistent with him conspiring with the claimant to cause an accident. The chances of them proving that are, of course, negligible but the hope is that an unsympathetic judge might take against the claimant and find in the defendant's favour.

Parallel Cars

This is the situation where the two cars are travelling alongside each other and one or other of them moves slightly sideways encroaching into the other vehicle's lane. Sometimes that happens because a driver is changing lanes negligently and has not seen the other vehicle (perhaps because it was in his blind spot), sometimes it occurs because one party is overtaking inappropriately and has to cut in. Often the scrape marks on the two vehicles become relevant because they can be used to show the relevant speeds of the two vehicles and in particular which was travelling more quickly and thus passing the other. Again, the question of what a driver saw, the distances travelled, the speed, the time involved and the like will be critical.

Oncoming Cars

This is either a straightforward scenario where there is sufficient room for the two vehicles to pass under normal circumstances and one driver has encroached onto the other side of the road, or the more difficult situation where there is in fact insufficient room for the two vehicles to pass. In the former case one might reasonably look at the layout of the road, particularly if the accident occurred on a bend, to see which vehicle is more likely to have strayed from the proper line. The latter case often occurs on blind bends on windy country roads and can cause the court some difficulty. The starting point in many a judicial mind is that such cases are 50/50 where both parties are equally to blame. That is wrong. The starting point is to determine whether either driver was in fact negligent. If one vehicle is significantly larger than the other, such that it automatically encroaches into the oncoming lane, the onus will be on that driver to ensure that oncoming traffic is safe. The mere fact that an oncoming vehicle is unable to avoid him does not mean that both parties are to blame. If and only if both parties are at fault to some extent will the court need to consider apportionment and there is a risk that by considering the most likely endpoint as the starting point the court will fall into error.[1]

---

1   E.g. *Gray v Gibson* [2014] EWCA Civ 355

Vehicle Exiting a Side Road

In most cases, this sort of scenario is fairly clear-cut: the vehicle on the main road normally has right of way and, whilst the emerging driver might aver that he took all reasonable care, had a restricted view, did not emerge fully, or that the other driver was driving too quickly, the onus on the emerging driver is a high one. Ironically, the problem often arises because the emerging driver is too cautious in his manoeuvre rather than reckless. There can, however, be circumstances where the emerging car cannot be blamed. If, for instance, the road layout is such that it would be impossible to detect the approaching car (e.g. because it would be around the bend and out of sight at the point of the manoeuvre) the emerging vehicle may escape liability. There would, however, need to be relatively compelling evidence to suggest that there was nothing more that the emerging vehicle could have done. Thinking time will be important here.

Another argument for drivers emerging is that their view was restricted by vehicles negligently parked on the corner. The difficulty of course is that one has to identify the person who has parked negligently and also prove that that was causative. From the point of view of the person on the main road they are normally able to blame the emerging driver at least to a material degree and thus recover in full.

These cases will depend on sightlines, speed and road position and both sides should look carefully at photographs of the junction, taking measurements if necessary to prove their respective points. The use of Internet images is now commonplace and the court will normally direct that the parties agree a plan and photographs of the accident location before trial.

The last type of case under this heading is that where the vehicle on the main road has given a misleading signal, suggesting an intention to turn into that side road from which the other driver is emerging. Sometimes this allegation is made without any foundation, sometimes the driver is signalling because the indicator has not cancelled, sometimes the vehicle has slowed either because the driver had intended to turn to the side road or, perhaps, because he intended to pull into the left-hand side immediately beyond the side road. Whilst there are inevitably questions of fact in such cases there can be a finding of contributory negligence against the driver from the main road who gives the misleading signal, normally in the region of one third.

Oncoming Vehicle Turning Across the Other Vehicle's Path

This accident happens remarkably regularly, either because the driver executing the manoeuvre thinks that they have more time than they actually have, hasn't actually seen the approaching vehicle for whatever reason or believes that the manoeuvre is legitimate, perhaps because of traffic signals. This is particularly prevalent where there is a filter light which would give the turning driver the right of way when illuminated. In cases such as this the order of the traffic lights can become important. If, for instance, the filter light does not illuminate until the oncoming traffic's lights have turned to red, the oncoming vehicle has potentially passed through a red light and would be liable for the accident. Of course, the turning vehicle may have taken advantage of a green light for that traffic on its side of the carriageway intending to travel straight ahead to move towards the centre of the junction in the hope of making its turn as soon as possible. In those circumstances, one occasionally sees a situation where, having moved to the middle of the junction, the turning vehicle then jumped the gun and executed the turn before determining whether it was safe to do so.

If the filter light comes on at the start of the phase, when both vehicles would normally have been stopped, the turning vehicle will normally have right of way (because the filter will turn green before the oncoming light changes). That said, why would the oncoming vehicle then set off on a red light? The answer is normally that the filter light has been illuminated for some time, has been extinguished, and that the turning driver has attempted his manoeuvre when in fact he no longer has right of way. That does not necessarily exonerate the oncoming driver because a green light only means go when it is safe to go, but the turning driver may struggle in those circumstances.

One can normally obtain a phasing diagram of the junction from the local authority, or, if necessary, a witness (often an engineer) can attend the scene and take suitable measurements. From a litigator's point of view, it is important to bear in mind the concept of thinking time. Where was the oncoming vehicle a second or two before impact? Did it have the opportunity to stop at the lights?

Roundabouts

It is an interesting question as to whether traditional roundabouts or mini roundabouts pose more of a potential problem for drivers. On a traditional roundabout the difficulty is that the two vehicles are travelling in parallel, but manoeuvring around a bend, whilst each looking to exit the roundabout at some point. The matter is inevitably made more complicated by people describing the left-hand lane as the outside lane (because it is the outside of the roundabout) whereas in traditional parlance the outside lane (on a straight road) is the right hand lane. As a litigator, drafting a witness statement to use left lane and right lane will avoid those difficulties.

The real question on a standard, traditional, roundabout is whether the car in the right hand lane is entitled to move across the left-hand lane so as to exit the roundabout and/or whether the car in the left-hand lane is entitled to remain on the roundabout in circumstances where the lane in question inevitably filters off to that exit. Again, photographs are important, as are any marks on the vehicles which will tend to suggest the relative movement between the two cars at impact. If one car is moving faster than the other, is that because the other vehicle was braking or is it because the first vehicle was accelerating? What does that tell us about the actions of the respective drivers at the material time?

Mini roundabouts pose their own problems because the nature of such a junction is that one might reasonably expect vehicles to be approaching from one or more of the roads so governed and there is inevitably a risk that a vehicle on the supposedly main road will continue straight across, either because the driver has not appreciated the mini roundabout in time or because simply looking to one's right (to see if one has to give way to a vehicle already established) might mean that one is oblivious to vehicles entering from the left. The proximity of the various different roads means that vehicles entering a mini roundabout might well do so immediately ahead of another vehicle. There is also the potential problem of vehicles cutting across the mini roundabout either because of laziness or the road layout.

A good proportion of accidents at mini roundabouts arise because one driver or the other mistakenly believes that he has right of way because of the road from which he approaches as opposed to whether or not he is the first vehicle onto the roundabout. This is normally a question of fact.

Opening Door of Parked Car

A surprising number of accidents are caused by somebody in a parked car opening their door so that a passing vehicle collides with it. The person opening the door is clearly under a duty to ensure that it is safe to do so and in general terms one might reasonably exit the vehicle from the pavement side if that is safer. Obviously, the driver is likely to exit the vehicle via his own door, but has the benefit of his wing mirror and/or to look over your shoulder to ensure that it is safe to do so. Equally, the driver of the moving vehicle should keep a safe distance between his line of travel and parked cars. If the door is only open by very short distance, why is the moving car hitting it? If the door is open to a significant degree, the impact potentially pulls the door further open and could rip it off its hinges and this is potentially a useful tool in determining the extent to which the person in the stationary vehicle had opened the door before the accident.

One point to bear in mind in such cases is that the policy of motor insurance applying to the stationary vehicle is unlikely to cover the acts or omissions of passengers as opposed to the driver. It might be possible to argue that the driver was negligent in pulling up at that location and thus requiring or permitting his passenger to open the door negligently but that is not an easy argument to run. It is also worth bearing in mind that such accidents tend to occur in relatively narrow roads at relatively low speeds and there tend to be arguments as to whether any injury can be caused at all.

Single Vehicle Accidents

There are a number of circumstances where an accident occurs with only one vehicle involved. The driver may have been driving too quickly and/or have lost control. He may have swerved to avoid a hazard such as an animal or a pedestrian. There may have been a mechanical failure.

Without an unforeseeable mechanical problem the driver will normally struggle to avoid liability. The chances are that had he been keeping a proper lookout or driving more carefully he would be able to act differently so as to avoid the accident which ultimately occurred. That said, there are clearly circumstances where one could not foresee the hazard arising and could reasonably expect to be absolved of blame. A pedestrian running across the road some distance ahead might reasonably be expected to have cleared the road before the vehicle reaches that point, but if he trips and falls, meaning that the driver, rather than having simply to slow down, has to brake to a halt to avoid running him over, claims by the driver's passengers might not meet with judicial sympathy.

If there has been a mechanical failure, the question will inevitably arise as to whether the driver could or should have identified the potential problem in good time. A bald tyre should be detected in good time. One would normally expect a driver to realise there was a problem with his brakes before having to apply them in emergency circumstances. A blowout on the tyre, however, might occur without negligence. Again it will be a question of fact.

Conclusion

The various scenarios set out should emphasise that road traffic litigation is very fact sensitive. Whilst the legal authorities give helpful guidance they are rarely determinative. Accurate witness statements, good photographs, engineering evidence if appropriate, and face-to-face (if possible) discussion with the driver will all maximise one's chances of success at trial. What a driver could see and do at any given point in time will almost always be critical and it is naïve to think that one can simply engage in road traffic litigation "by numbers". That said, a little thought and analysis will normally go a long way.

PART THREE

PUBLIC LIABILITY CLAIMS

CHAPTER EIGHT
THE LEGAL ISSUES

Whilst technically a public liability claim is any claim whereby a member of the public suffers injury, such that the phrase will include claims of negligence, the more normal circumstances for public liability claims involve the state of the premises or land where the accident occurs. These claims are often referred to as "slips and trips" and normally involve people falling and thereby sustaining injury. Equally, accidents where objects fall on people will often come into this category and there are various other means by which members of the public might come to harm.

The starting point, as in any other personal injury claim, is the duty of care. The existence of a duty and the nature of that duty will depend on the precise circumstances of the case, starting with the nature of the area in question and the claimant's right to be there. The historical development of the law in this area forms part of the academic study rather than the practical reality. The existence and extent of the duty is normally governed by one of the various Acts of Parliament set out below, albeit that there is always the scope for a residual claim in negligence or perhaps nuisance.

Occupiers' Liability Act 1957

The simplest form of public liability claim is normally one under the Occupiers' Liability Act 1957. This Act governs the legal relationship between the owner/occupier of land on the one hand and lawful visitors to those premises on the other. Section 1 of the Act identifies the occupier as the person controlling the premises, and thus in the best position to identify and prevent the risk of harm to lawful visitors. More than one person can be an occupier under the Act and therefore a claimant might well be owed a duty of care by more than one defendant. This can, of course, be important where one or other of the potential tortfeasors is not in a position to satisfy a judgment.

The important issue is that the claimant must be a lawful visitor to the premises. The reasons for his being there are not relevant, as long as his presence there is lawful. Unlawful visitors, or trespassers, are not owed a duty of care under this Act, but see the Occupiers Liability Act 1984 below.

Importantly, the Act relates to the state of premises rather than the activities being carried out on those premises. That means that where the danger arises from what is being done or the way in which it is being done the Act does not normally assist the claimant who will have to rely on common law negligence principles. There can be overlap: if for instance a defendant spills fluid on a staircase which has no effective draining facility, the spillage itself is a negligent act, the failure to clean the spillage is a potentially negligent omission, and the design of the staircase might be a defect in the state of the premises for the purposes of the Act.[1]

The duty is on the occupier to take such care as in all the circumstances is reasonable to see that the visitor will be reasonably safe in using the premises for the purposes for which he is invited or permitted to be there. This last restriction means that an occupier can limit the nature of the activities which the visitor might undertake on the premises, or limit his access to certain parts of the premises. The overriding issue is that this is a test of reasonableness – it is not an absolute duty to keep the visitor safe.

The Act requires an occupier to be prepared for children to be less careful than adults and thus potentially imposes a higher duty in respect of such visitors. Equally, the Act allows a lower duty of care in respect of those visiting the premises in the exercise of their calling, because professionals, entering the premises to undertake their work, might reasonably appreciate the dangers which come about because of those matters which demand their expertise in the first place.

In reality, both of these clarifications of the duty to be owed represent extensions of what is and isn't reasonable. If dealing with the hazard is beyond the competence and expertise of the occupier and he calls in a

---

1 C.f. Regulations 12(1) and 12(3) of the Workplace (Health, Safety and Welfare) Regulations 1992, dealt with in Chapter 10 below.

professional to do the job for him, he has acted reasonably. If a child is particularly vulnerable, more care will be required to keep them safe.

What then is reasonable in all the normal circumstances? A warning sign might suffice if, on its own, that would allow the visitor to be reasonably safe, although where a danger is extreme or unusual a warning sign may be insufficient. Sometimes a barrier or additional notice needs to be placed. Equally, where a danger is obvious, there is not normally a need for warning signs. Whilst there are a number of Appellate cases on what might render premises hazardous and whether an occupier has fulfilled his duty of care, they tend to be fact sensitive. That is not to say that one should not research similar cases as and when the need arises, just that they need not be learnt or set out here.

The Act also establishes that an occupier is not liable, without more, where the hazard arises as a result of faulty execution of any work of construction, maintenance or repair by an independent contractor. The question in those cases comes down to whether the contractor is of apparent good repute and/or whether the occupier has confirmed the work has been properly done.

Occupiers Liability Act 1984

The 1957 Act governs the situation where the claimant is a lawful visitor. The 1984 Act creates a potential duty of care to a trespasser. There are two issues: first as to whether a duty of care is owed at all and second the nature of that duty. The duty is owed if the occupier (a) is aware of the danger or has reasonable grounds to believe that it exists; (b) he knows or has reasonable grounds to believe that the claimant is in the vicinity of the danger concerned or that he may come into the vicinity of the danger (in either case, whether the claimant has lawful authority for being in that vicinity or not); and (c) the risk is one against which, in all the circumstances of the case, he may reasonably be expected to offer the claimant some protection.

If, and only if, those three elements are satisfied does the occupier owe a duty to take such care as is reasonable in all the circumstances to see that the claimant does not suffer injury on the premises by reason of the danger concerned. That duty can be discharged by taking such steps as are reasonable in all the circumstances to give a warning of the danger concerned or to discourage persons from incurring the risk. No duty is owed to a claimant who willingly accepts those risks.

In other words, if you are the occupier of land and you know that the land is potentially hazardous and you know that the claimant is likely to come into contact with the hazard and the risk to the claimant of coming into contact with that hazard warrants it then you are under an obligation to take reasonable steps to warn of that danger or to discourage him from incurring the risk. The case law covers each of those three steps to the imposition of a duty as well as whether the occupier has complied with the same.

Defective Premises Act 1972

Both of the above Acts stem from the fact that the occupier has day-to-day control over the premises and thus is able to identify potential hazards and repair or remedy them. The Defective Premises Act operates to impose a duty upon a landlord of premises. The nature of the lease will normally allow the tenant to control access to the premises and, moreover, will give the tenant himself access to the premises as of right. That means that he is no mere visitor, nor is the landlord obliged to be proactive in his maintenance of the premises. Indeed, the hazard might arise from the tenant's use of the premises.

The 1972 Act creates a duty of care, once more to take such care as is reasonable in all the circumstances, in respect of any relevant defect. A relevant defect means a defect which existed at or after the commencement of the tenancy which is within the knowledge of the landlord (whether as a result of being notified by the tenant or otherwise) or if the landlord in all the circumstances ought to have known of the relevant defect.

Such cases therefore turn on the question of notice and the extent to which the landlord should have availed himself of any opportunity to inspect and repair or maintain the premises. Most landlords keep records of complaints and will survey the premises before the commencement of any tenancy for precisely this purpose.

Highways Act 1980

Each of the above Acts centres on the fact that the party owing the duty has control over the premises themselves and, potentially, the claimant's use thereof, but the law of highways is different. The highway is a public right of way. Each and every member of the public potentially has the right to use the highway without restriction. They are not visitors, nor are they trespassers: they are there as of right. Unlike the Defective Premises Act, there is no specific class of person who might visit or use the highway and the person responsible for the highway cannot take it back.

In those circumstances no duty is owed under the Occupiers' Liability Acts of 1957 or 1984, or under the Defective Premises Act 1972. Indeed, there is no duty owed at all at common law. The only circumstances where a user of the highway can bring a claim is where, pursuant to section 41 of the Highways Act 1980, the highway is maintainable at public expense. In those circumstances the local authority is under an obligation to maintain the highway (section 41), subject to it having a defence pursuant to section 58 of the same Act.

The duty is an absolute one to maintain the highway subject to the section 58 defence. That means that in order to succeed, a claimant must firstly prove that the highway was in a hazardous condition, secondly that that condition arose from a failure to maintain on the part of the local authority (as opposed to the acts or omissions of a third party), and thirdly that the hazardous nature of the highway caused the claimant's accident.

There have been a number of cases about what constitutes a danger in the highway. Whilst the courts have always stressed that there is no absolute test and that imperfections must be tolerated, as a general rule defects in excess of an inch or so are normally deemed hazardous to pedestrians. A little more tolerance is normally extended to defects within the carriageway.

Even if the claimant can prove those three matters to the satisfaction of the court, the defendant will still escape liability if it can show that it took such care as is reasonable in all circumstances to ensure that that part of the highway was not dangerous to traffic.

Section 58(2) identifies specific factors to which the court should have regard, being the character of the highway, the traffic which was reasonably expected to use it, the standard of maintenance appropriate for a highway of that character and used by such traffic, the state of repair in which a reasonable person would have expected to find the highway, whether the highway authority knew (or could reasonably have been expected to know) that the highway was in a dangerous condition, and/or the warning signs put in place (where the highway authority could not reasonably have been expected to conduct a repair before the accident).

With those matters in mind, most local authorities operate a system of inspection, maintenance and repair designed to identify hazards on the highway in good time and remedy the problem, or at least persuade the court that they were taking such steps as were reasonable in all the circumstances to keep the highway safe. The frequency of those inspections is normally set out in a policy document, as are the action levels whereby any putative hazard is deemed repairable and/or the appropriate timescale for repairs. Footpaths and carriageways may have different standards. A busy high street will probably be inspected more often than a back alley. Some locations will require inspection on foot, whilst some inspections will be carried out from a moving vehicle. Cases often turn on whether the defect has been missed on a previous inspection, or even a subsequent inspection, and whether or not an attempt to repair has been made. Defendants may choose not to repair the alleged defect, in an attempt to assert that it is insufficiently dangerous to warrant intervention. It is worth bearing in mind that the onus is on the defendant to prove its defence under section 58.

It follows that in highway claims the issues tend to be fairly straightforward: Was the highway dangerous? Did that cause the claimant to fall? Has the defendant got a proper system of inspection and maintenance in place?

Nuisance/Negligence

The last type of claim worth noting under this section is where, even if the claimant cannot show a defect in the state of the premises, he can identify an act, or occasionally omission, on the part of a defendant who has thereby caused that defect. Lorries leaving a building site might transfer gravel onto the highway rendering it dangerous. The owner of a shop might be liable should his signage fall and hit a pedestrian. The user of premises, being, in effect, an occupier can be liable to members of the public if his use of the premises unreasonably creates a danger or hazard. The lorry driver who repeatedly drives up onto the kerb, damaging it over time, creates a public nuisance and, if he can be identified, can be held liable for the resultant accident.

To put the above scenarios into context, imagine an alleyway at the end of a terraced street. The council, aware that bin lorries and other vehicles need to be able to turn, installs a turning area at the end of the street, demarcating that area with blocks set flush into the ground and tarmacking the area within the blocks. Over time, however, the unmade section of the alleyway on the far side of the blocks erodes, such that the blocks themselves form a tripping hazard. The street is a highway maintainable at public expense but the alleyway is not. There is no liability on the local authority under the Highways Act 1980 because the tripping hazard is on the unadopted section of the highway. There is no liability *qua* occupier because the alleyway has been in use for so long that it is a highway and the claimant is therefore there as of right. The original decision to place the blocks flush with the ground is not unreasonable and is not negligent. There is no obligation upon the highway authority to repair and maintain the area around, but outside, the blocks. The claimant would fail on each of those arguments. That said, why has the unadopted alleyway been eroded? If the claimant can show that the very bin wagons for which the turning circle was installed habitually overran the blocks onto the unmade road beyond, and, in so manoeuvring, ripped up the surface of the alleyway, then those vehicles were causative of a public nuisance. In circumstances where the refuse collectors are council employees, the local authority would ultimately be vicariously liable for the nuisance thus created and therefore, by a rather tortuous route, owe a duty of care to the claimant. Interestingly, in such a circumstance, the strength of the claimant's argument on the nuisance point is dependent in good part on the fact that the local authority would escape liability in any other circumstance.

Transient Defects

The above scenarios tend to centre on circumstances where the changes to the accident location are permanent in nature: a broken flagstone, a hole, a missing handrail. None of those will remedy itself in time. Indeed, the problem will normally get worse. Some hazards, however, are more transient in nature but are just as actionable, albeit normally in negligence rather than one or other of the Acts discussed above.

One exception is the duty imposed by section 41(1A) of the Highways Act 1980 which places a highway authority under a duty to ensure, so far as is reasonably practicable, that safe passage along the highway is not endangered by snow or ice. That amendment came about because in *Goodes v East Sussex County Council*[2] the House of Lords held that the requirement to maintain the highway did not extend to gritting it, meaning that Mr Goodes was not compensated when he lost control on an ungritted road sustaining injuries which rendered him almost entirely paralysed.

The wording of section 41(1A) still allows for a defendant to show that it was not reasonably practicable to prevent the accumulation of snow or ice and the question will still have to be determined by reference to all the circumstances of the case.

A more difficult scenario might arise where there is a build-up of, for instance, pigeon droppings, over time, rendering the surface of the highway slippery. Can that be said to have affected the surface so that the highway is no longer "maintained"? The defect is not permanent in the sense that it could be cleaned away, but is not transient in the sense that it will melt or otherwise disperse over time without direct action by an individual. The claimant would argue that changing the coefficient of friction of the highway rendered it dangerous, that such a change in circumstances should be apparent on inspection, and that a competent

---

2 [2000] UKHL 34

inspector would conclude the work had to be undertaken to maintain the highway and restore it to its original state. Public health concerns could also be raised. The defendant would argue that the highway itself had not fallen into disrepair, just that a substance had come to be on the surface, compromising that surface in the short term, akin to a spillage for which the highway authority would not be liable. Of course, a claimant would have to establish in the first instance that the pigeon droppings were the cause of his fall, failing which he would not be able to establish liability in any event.

Cases involving spillages and cleaning systems are dealt with in Part Four. Similar principles apply whatever the basis of the claim.

CHAPTER NINE
THE FACTUAL ISSUES

Does a duty apply? If so, what duty?

As will be clear from the above analysis, the starting point for any claim is to identify which, if any, Act or scenario applies and the identity of the relevant defendant. Having done that, the claimant will need to identify whether the requirements for a duty of care have been made out: in some cases the duties are self-proving whilst in others the claimant will have to prove it. In reality, the nature of the duty is normally one to take such care as is reasonable in all the circumstances, subject to whether the burden of proof falls on the defendant or the claimant.

Is there a prima facie breach of that duty?

This will normally come down to whether the location where the claimant sustained injury was, at the material time, dangerous. That is inevitably a question of fact for the court to determine, having regard to all the circumstances of the case. The case law may give guidance but is unlikely to be determinative.

Does the defendant have a defence?

Sometimes the Act itself provides a defence at law, but in reality there is normally a question of fact as to whether the defendant has acted reasonably and can therefore escape liability. Systems of inspection and repair, cleaning and maintenance and the like give a defendant a prospect of defending the claim. One does not need to record such inspections as a matter of law, but rather as a matter of evidencing the system and, normally, the absence of any defect on the last inspection prior to the accident. It is all too easy to mistake the need for paperwork as being part of the duty itself rather than simply evidencing what the defendant has done.

Did the hazard cause the claimant's accident?

This will be a question of fact and will normally come down to the claimant's credibility. There may, of course, be CCTV footage or an independent witness but the majority of such claims involve the claimant being put to proof of the circumstances of the accident. Unless the claimant can persuade the court that his version is correct, he will fail. This can be particularly unfair if for instance an entire footpath is in a poor state of repair such that no one defect can be identified as the cause of the fall, although that does not mean that the judge will reject the claimant's contention that the most actionable defect was the one which caused him to trip.

There can of course be circumstances where the claimant himself can't recall the precise circumstances of the accident (e.g. due to alcohol consumed) but a third party can fill in those gaps. Whether that witness is compelling is the question of the court having regard to their demeanour and the nature of their evidence. The witness who goes to help the claimant to his feet, believing the injury to be a sprained ankle, only to discover that the claimant has also broken his wrist, has the ring of truth.

Contributory Negligence

It goes without saying that the claimant who slips, trips or falls will potentially be penalised for failing to identify the hazard and avoiding it. The larger and more obvious the hazard the more likely a finding of contributory negligence and the greater the likely reduction. That, of course, will depend on all the circumstances of the case. Has the claimant had the opportunity to see the defect before? Did the claimant have the opportunity to see the defect on this occasion? A commuter, walking in a crowd, is unlikely to be able to look to the ground so as to see a defect, whereas, once the crowds have cleared, it might be obvious.

There is an irony in that the harder a defect is to detect (thus making it more difficult for the defendant to identify it and fix it), the lower the finding of contributory negligence in the event that the claimant can establish liability. The scenario where the defect is so large that the defendant had no excuse will normally lead to a more significant reduction for contributory negligence. As with motor claims it is a matter of balancing moral turpitude and causative potency.

Conclusion

Public liability claims have been a mainstay of personal injury litigation for many years. The majority of injuries sustained are relatively modest as one might expect. Because of the element of reasonableness in determining whether a defendant is liable or not there is an element of zeitgeist in the court's attitude to such litigation. In the 1990s local authorities struggled to win cases under the Highways Act 1980: their systems were the subject of close inspection and failures to comply with maintenance regimes far in excess of what might reasonably have been required were deemed to be failures sufficient to render the defendant liable. More recently, the politics of compensation culture on the one hand and austerity on the other have come into play, and the fact that a defendant cannot operate a perfect system has become a less likely reason to fix them with liability. What is reasonable has to take into account *all* the circumstances of the case.

PART FOUR

EMPLOYERS' LIABILITY CLAIMS

CHAPTER TEN
THE LEGAL ISSUES

Despite (some would say because of) the advent of health and safety in the workplace, claims arising from injuries sustained in the course of employment remain commonplace. Historically, workplaces involved manual work, machinery, time pressure and an imbalance in power between the employer and the workforce. The industrial revolution meant that factory owners could make significant profits whilst labour was cheap. The advent of unionisation and workers' rights over the years represents both cause and effect in a shift in attitudes in the workplace and in wider society.

Accident or Disease?

There are two types of claim which can arise from one's employment. The first is the traditional accident at work where a specific event befalls the claimant leaving him injured. He might slip or trip over something which should not have been there. He might lift an excessively heavy weight and hurt himself. His protective equipment (if any) might fail so that he suffers a trauma which might otherwise have been avoided. A machine might malfunction causing him to injure himself. He might simply manage to injure himself through his own failure to appreciate that he was putting himself in a dangerous position, perhaps as a result of a failure of his training.

The second type of case is where the working conditions themselves, to which the claimant is exposed over a period of time, cause, by dint of that (repetitive) exposure, the claimant to suffer injury. The failing is not a one-off which gives rise to trauma, but a systemic problem. Whether that exposure is to a pathogen, excessive noise, repetitive movement or even stress at work, the injury arises as a result of the employer's conduct over a period of time. This sort of injury is often referred to as a disease case.

In reality, there is often very little to choose between the traditional claim for traumatic injury and disease litigation. The main difference arises where the disease which the claimant develops is a divisible, cumulative, condition as discussed in chapter 5 above. Importantly, the majority of such conditions are relatively commonplace so that one knows from the outset whether this is a case of divisible or indivisible injury. Sometimes, however, a relatively common condition can be said to have arisen from a relatively unusual cause (e.g. excessive exposure to vibrating tools can cause Vibration White Finger, a divisible condition which normally comes on by degrees, but what if the claimant actually develops Carpal Tunnel Syndrome that using vibrating tools? That is an unusual outcome requiring clear medical evidence on the question of causation).

Employment

It is worth discussing, briefly, the concept of employment. The layman has a fairly clear understanding of what employment might constitute. The employee who arrives at the factory gates at 8.00am and works his shift until the sirens signal that he and his colleagues can go home is under no illusion that he is not an employee, but work is now a far more flexible concept, with recruitment companies supplying short-term labour to employers, whose contract is with the recruitment company supplying the individual, not the individual supplying the labour. Equally, the taxation system allows individuals to be self-employed for the purposes of taxation and National Insurance contributions, even if they work in the same place, for the same foreman, for months at a time.

It would, of course, be anomalous if two workers, one in the direct employ of the company and another who, on paper, was contracted to a company who did nothing more than supply his labour to the company, were owed different duties of care.

The answer[1] is that the law looks at the *de facto* situation to decide whether the individual is, in reality, an employee or an independent contractor. The test is one of control. There is a difference between straight-forward labourers who attend site, perhaps with some of their own generic tools, and specialist sub-contractors, who bring their own specialist equipment with them. Who tells the individual how to do the

---

1 *Lane v The Shire Roofing Company (Oxford) Limited* [1995] EWCA Civ 37

job? If the putative employer has that level of control, the individual is likely to be treated as an employee, whatever his tax status. The Court of Appeal in *Lane* posed the question: "Whose business was it?" and answered that question by saying that it was the respondent's business, he should have supplied the scaffold necessary to allow the appellant claimant the means to undertake the work safely, and duly owed a duty of care.

Duty of Care

The common law imposes upon an employer a duty to take reasonable care for the safety of each of his employees. That duty extends to providing a safe place of work, a safe system of work, competent work colleagues, and safe work equipment. It is a duty in negligence where the onus is on the claimant to show that his employer fell short.

That means that, particularly in disease cases, a question inevitably arises as to what the employer should have known at any given point in time about the risks posed by his operation. That in turn means that the state of knowledge of the industry as a whole needs to be considered (because that is what might reasonably be expected of a normal employer of that type) but one must also consider whether a particular employer, for instance a large, market leading, company would have had particular knowledge and understanding before that information had trickled down into the wider public domain. The starting point is often published research papers or government guidance. Because the diseases in question have been the subject of significant litigation over the years, there is normally a widely accepted date of knowledge which the courts will impose upon defendants so that any exposure to the relevant risk after that point will normally be deemed to have been negligent.

Over time, Parliament passed various Acts introducing statutory provisions to govern how employers treat their employees. The Factories Act 1961 consolidated previous Factories Acts and enactments relating to the safety, health and welfare of employed persons. It is an interesting snapshot of the workplace 50 years ago. Nevertheless, the duty of care on employer was still one of reasonableness in all the circumstances.

The Health and Safety at Work etc. Act 1974 was the next significant development in the legislation. The preamble identifies it as *"An Act to make further provision for securing the health, safety and welfare, for protecting others against risks to health or safety in connection with the activities of persons at work, for controlling the keeping in use and preventing the unlawful acquisition, possession and use of dangerous substances, and for controlling certain emissions into the atmosphere; to make further provision with respect to the employment medical advisory service; to amend the law relating to building regulations, and the Building (Scotland) Act 1959; and for connected purposes."* Perhaps most importantly for this book, section 47 of the Act provided that a breach of statutory duty gave rise to civil liability.

Section 2 of that Act sets out the general duties of employers to their employees and makes it clear that it shall be the duty of every employer to ensure, so far as is reasonably practicable, the health, safety and welfare at work of all his employees. It makes it clear that an employer's duties include:

(a) the provision and maintenance of plant and systems of work that are, so far as is reasonably practicable, safe and without risks to health;

(b) arrangements for ensuring the safety and absence of risks to health in connection with the use, handling, storage and transport of articles and substances;

(c) the provision of such information, instruction, training and supervision as is necessary to ensure, so far as is reasonably practicable, health and safety at work of his employees;

(d) so far as is reasonably practicable as regards the place of work under the employer's control, the maintenance of it in a condition that is safe and without risks to health and the provision and maintenance of means access to and egress from it that are safe and without such risks;

(e) the provision and maintenance of a working environment for his employees that is, so far as is reasonably practicable, safe, without risks to health, and adequate as regards facilities and arrangements for their welfare at work.

The concept of reasonable practicability puts on the defendant a burden of proof to show that, in effect, he could not do more. Clearly, some things might be beyond his control, but the Act put the onus on the employer to keep his employees safe.

The Act also requires every employer to prepare, and as often as may be appropriate, revise a written statement of his general policy with respect to the health and safety at work of his employees. Parliament was putting the health and safety of employees, and non-employees who nevertheless worked in the same premises, or used the same equipment, at the heart of the legislation.

The next step came in the late 1980s/early 1990s when various sets of Regulations were introduced which further defined the obligations of employers, breach of which obligations potentially amounted to an offence under the Health and Safety at Work etc. Act 1974, but, more importantly, also giving employees a civil right of action for breach of statutory duty. Whilst the traditional reference is to the 'Six Pack'[2], the Noise at Work Regulations 1989, which came into force on 1 January 1990, beat them to punch.

---

2 It's always a good test to ask people to name the six sets of Regulations which make up the original Six Pack, firstly because the majority of people really struggle to recall more than 3 or 4 pieces of data in one block in any event, and secondly because there only 5 of them are commonly seen. The complete list is the Management (Health, Safety and Welfare) Regulations 1992 (now 1999), the Provision and Use of Work Equipment Regulations 1992 (now 1998), the Manual Handling Operations Regulations 1992, the Workplace (Health, Safety and Welfare) Regulations 1992, the Personal Protective Equipment at Work Regulations 1992 and the Health and Safety (Display Screen Equipment) Regulations 1992. The Control of Substances Hazardous to Health Regulations 2002 and Work at Height Regulations 2005 are among the late arrivals at the party. There are several more, governing various aspects of health and safety in the workplace and beyond. The HSE website sets out a full list.

There are various purposes to this sort of statutory instrument: The first, although perhaps so obvious that people don't notice it, is to identify that there are certain aspects of the world of employment which pose a potential, albeit generic, risk to employees. The second is to set out the specific risks which need to be considered within that area of specialism. The third is to identify, if possible, some sort of objective standard to which the employer falls to be held. Those standards fall to be changed from time to time as our understanding, or perception of risk, alters. Many of the standards in question emanate from European Union standards. Finally, they set out the level of the duty to be imposed on the employer. Is it a duty of reasonableness, to take all reasonably practicable steps, or is it an absolute duty, where even a blame-free technical breach is still a breach?

The first purpose is normally apparent from the title of the statutory instrument in question. The mere fact that the Management of Health, Safety and Welfare at work warrants a set of regulations should put an employer on notice that systems and working practices are just as important as specific instructions about specific tasks. It should be obvious that moving large, heavy or dangerous items poses a risk to the individual[3]. Working with pathogens should be a fairly obvious risk, as should be the risk of excessive exposure to noise or vibration, but the very fact that there is specific guidance puts the employer on full and proper notice that this is an area of work which requires some sort of surveillance, consideration and input to keep workers safe.

Once the generic area of risk has been identified, the specific regulations deal with different aspects. The Workplace (Health, Safety and Welfare) Regulations 1992, for instance, start by identifying what might constitute a workplace and then require an employer not just to maintain it, but to clean it, ventilate it, light it, protect people working within it and provide them with basic facilities, such as washing and sanitary facilities and drinking water. In the 21st century, we take such matters as a given, and bemoan the fact that workers in other countries

---

3 Although the writer recently saw an averment that two men trying to wheel a half-tonne x-ray machine off the back of a delivery lorry using the tail-gate lift was not, in fact, a manual handling operation, even after it fell on the man below.

do not have those rights, whilst simultaneously, it appears, bemoaning 'red tape'.

The objective standards which might be set under the regulations are important. The risk of exposure to excessive noise, vibration, asbestos or the like, has been known about in general terms for many years, but what level of exposure is safe? This goes back to the question of an employer's knowledge, referred to above. If the established theory at any given point in time is that a certain level of exposure represents a safe level, but that understanding changes and it is realised that the previously recommended level was nevertheless dangerous, the employer falls to be judged by the standards of the relevant time not the current state of thinking.

Perhaps the most interesting aspect of the regulations is the standard required of the employer. It was well understood that employers had to take reasonable care, but more stringent standards appear on the face of these statutory instruments, specifically 'reasonable practicability' and the strict 'shall (ensure)'.

A useful comparison of the two might be regulation 12 of the Workplace (Health, Safety and Welfare) Regulations 1992:

> *12(1) Every floor in a workplace ... shall be of a construction such that the floor ... is suitable for the purpose for which it is used.*
>
> *12(3) So far as is reasonably practicable, every floor in a workplace ... shall be kept free from obstructions and from any article or substance which may cause a person to slip, trip or fall.*

The former requirement is an absolute requirement, and it is easy to see why. Construction has an element of permanence to it. If one is putting in a floor, it has to be safe. The latter, however, has a dynamic and temporal aspect – an obstruction, article or substance, whilst it could be long-standing, is not normally part of the construction itself, and a spillage can happen seconds before the accident occurs.

The main effect of a requirement of reasonable practicability is to shift the burden of proof to the employer to show that it had done everything that was reasonably practicable to avoid the situation arising. That is a difficult test to satisfy on a micro-level, because if one ignores everything else that might be going on in a workplace and asks the specific question "Could you not have done X to avoid Y happening?", where the question is phrased with the hindsight that Y has, in fact, happened because X was not done, the answer is normally positive, but there remains the argument that Y was not foreseeable in advance, so that it was not practicable to avoid that which one did not foresee, or that the wider picture meant that it was reasonably practicable to do X for any given possible occurrence of Y. A cleaning system in a huge building cannot clean everywhere at once, and if workers have access to all parts of the building, 24 hours per day, one cannot, on a practicable level, avoid the possibility of workers coming into contact with the cleaners, nor is it possible to physically prevent access to the very specific area where the cleaners are operating without a constantly moving perimeter with people keeping lookout to prevent unauthorised entry. The best laid plans to ensure safety can, of course, fail, where, for instance, the positioning of Wet Floor signs at either end of the corridor being cleaned is not obvious to a person entering the area from a side room.

The interpretation of the requirement that an employer 'shall' or 'shall ensure'[4] was the subject of the Court of Appeal's decision in *Stark v The Post Office*[5] where the question distilled to this: If the employer provided the employee with work equipment (a bicycle) which failed through no fault of the employer, who had a programme of maintenance and could not be expected to prevent that failure, was the employer in breach of the statutory duty ('shall ensure') when that failure occurred?

The answer, the Court held, was yes. Whilst the Regulations had been brought in to implement an EU Directive on the matter, the regulation

---

4 E.g. Regulation 5(1) of the Provision and Use of Work Equipment Regulations 1998: Every employer shall ensure that work equipment is maintained in an efficient state, in efficient working order and in good repair.

5 [2000] EWCA Civ 64

was drafted to go further and to impose an absolute duty on the employer and The Post Office were liable for the injuries which Mr Stark suffered when his bicycle failed.

Is that fair? Should an employer who tries to maintain his work equipment still be liable to his employee through no fault of his own? The alternative question might be: Is it fair to the employee who goes to work, is told to use a piece of equipment, and who then sustains nasty injuries when that equipment fails, should not be entitled to compensation because he cannot show that his employer was negligent? In judging what is fair in all the circumstances, one might reasonably take into account that (a) the employer is under a legal obligation to carry insurance cover for his employees, but the employee is unlikely to hold equivalent cover for himself; and (b) there is a benefit for all concerned to have certainty, particularly when there is a move towards avoiding unnecessary litigation taking up court resources.

Nevertheless, tucked away at section 69 of the Enterprise and Regulatory Reform Act 2013[6], the Coalition government amended section 47 of the 1974 Act, removing the claimant's automatic right to compensation for a breach of statutory duty. This fundamental shift in workers' rights, introduced under the auspices of a reduction in red tape, removed, at a stroke, a central pillar of the protection offered to workers injured at work. Whilst the section allows for civil liabilities to be expressly created, nonesuch have been so far.[7]

It is not easy to discern a legal or moral basis for the provision being included. In the majority of cases, the strict liability under *Stark* (with which employers had dealt for 13 years without difficulty) simply represented a simpler, more definitive route to compensating the injured individual who might want to concentrate their concerns on rehabilitation and recovery rather than fighting to prove that their

---

6 In the Miscellaneous section of the Miscellaneous Chapter, between Inspection plans under the Regulatory Enforcement and Sanctions Act 2008 and Estate agency work, although given that the provision was apparently added at the eleventh hour, without, for instance, the Law Commission being asked to report, one should not have expected too much.

7 It would be simple enough to create a *Stark* exception were one motivated so to do.

injuries were caused by negligence on the part of their employer. The benefits of the provision are not yet clear, unless one subscribes to the view that this is just another attempt by non-lawyers to drive injured claimants from the courts (see Chapter 19). Certainly there were those who claimed, not without justification, that section 69 took health and safety law back by 100 years (and certainly back to 1973).

Against that background, the current state of the law is that old fashioned negligence principles apply, and that an employer's breach of a statutory duty is not determinative of whether there is a civil liability, even if it might be good evidence to that effect.

CHAPTER ELEVEN
THE FACTUAL ISSUES

What happened?

As the previous chapter makes clear, the onus is now on the claimant to prove that his employer was negligent in allowing or causing him to be injured. He will need to prove what happened, and why, before he can establish liability.

It is worth bearing in mind that the relationship between employer and employee means that employers' liability claims have a slightly different dynamic to road traffic accidents and public liability claims. The parties have had dealings, good or bad, potentially for several years if not decades before the claimant sustained his injury. The employee may have particular loyalty to the employer or be disgruntled. He may be fearful for his job. Witnesses may have similar concerns.

Those issues can pose problems when bringing a claim, but can also interfere with the smooth defence of the claim. The rule of three for defendants suddenly takes on a particular significance, because an employer might be fearful that a successful claim by this claimant will lead to a raft of similar claims from the rest of the workforce.

Against that background, the need for objective evidence, particularly contemporaneous evidence, takes on a new significance. Did the claimant report the accident? If so, what was said in the accident report? Did the employer complete a RIDDOR[1] form? Did the claimant have any input into the contents of that form? Was he interviewed and asked to provide his own version of events? What state was he in when he was interviewed? What do the hospital or ambulance notes say about what happened?

---

1 The Reporting of Injuries, Diseases and Dangerous Occurrence Regulations 2013 requires reporting for a wide range of injuries (excluding trivial injuries) or where a person at work is incapacitated for routine work for more than seven consecutive days excluding the day of the accident under Regulation 4. Regulation 8 contains an equivalent provision for Occupational diseases.

Clearly, in disease cases, there is unlikely to be a contemporaneous record, although from time to time historic records exist. Photographs of visiting dignitaries might show employees wearing all of their personal protective equipment, (perhaps noticeably newly distributed) or show the layout of the premises at the relevant time. They might give clues as to who was working there at the time, opening up new fields of enquiry.

Does a duty apply? If so, what duty?

As will be clear from the discussion in Chapter 11, the starting point for any claim is to identify which, if any, Act or scenario applies and the identity of the relevant defendant. Whether any breach of duty is sufficient to found a claim in negligence will depend on the facts of the case, but the starting point must still be to consider what the defendant should have been doing in terms of providing the claimant with a safe workplace and plant, a safe system of work and safe fellow employees. Which of those (and it may be more than one) is the reason for the claimant's injury?

Is there a prima facie breach of that duty?

As discussed, a breach of duty will often be good evidence of negligence. In cases of unsafe workplaces or plant, the failure of equipment is still a good place from which to start when it comes to showing that the defendant could and should have done more, although that will no longer be self-proving.

In cases of unsafe systems of work, the starting point will be the risk assessments and the method statements created before the accident, together with the documentation in support of the training provided. It may be that the claimant simply did not understand the training, either because it wasn't good enough, or because it was so complex that the key point was lost in the detail. Sometimes an employee will understand the words used to mean something else. When one reads a sentence as clearly holding the meaning you wish it to mean, it can be hard to see the alternative point of view. When the manual says: "Don't work under this piece of equipment without blocking it off" the employer may not appreciate that his field engineer perceives his efforts to diagnose the problem as being separate from actually repairing it, and not as "working" under the equipment.

Does the defendant have a defence?

This will depend on the precise facts of the case. Systems of inspection and repair, cleaning and maintenance and the like now give a defendant a prospect of defending the claim in negligence. Whilst the Regulations might require proper records, that will no longer be dispositive and, as with PL cases, such records will go to evidencing the system and, normally, the absence of any defect on the last inspection prior to the accident.

There is relatively little case law since the Enterprise and Regulatory Reform Act 2013 came into force. In time, if claimants cannot rely on a simple analysis of what went wrong on the occasion in question, greater emphasis will have to be laid on the systems in place and the training provided.

What caused the claimant's accident? Was there contributory negligence?

Because the accident occurred in the course of the claimant's employment, he may well have come across the same situation before. In the context of bringing a claim for negligence, the claimant's own actions will almost inevitably fall to be considered. What has changed from the last time he performed this task? Did the equipment just happen to fail this time? Did he simply get lucky on previous occasions? If the employee has to get to a tap 20 times a day and there are scaffolding poles lying on the floor immediately in front of it, he will eventually, almost inevitably, miss his footing and fall. That's a simple enough question of blameworthiness – they shouldn't have been there, he was aware of the hazard, and should have taken extra care. It is, however, a little unfair to suggest that he should have downed tools until they were moved or taken it upon himself to remove the hazard without assistance.

It goes without saying that the claimant who slips, trips or falls at work will potentially be penalised for failing to identify the hazard and avoiding it, just as in the PL situation. The comments in that chapter hold true: The larger and more obvious the hazard, the more likely a finding of contributory negligence and the greater the likely reduction. That, of course, will depend on all the circumstances of the case. Has the claimant had the opportunity to see the defect before? Did the claimant have the opportunity to see the defect on this occasion?

Disease claims

It is worth repeating that in disease claims, the starting point will be the specific duty owed at that point in time and showing (particularly in the case of cumulative conditions) the extent to which each employer was in causative breach of duty, so that his proportion of the claimant's damage can be assessed. This need not be on a simple time basis, as if the claimant works long hours with one employer for 10 years and shorter hours with another for 20 years, the overall effect may be the same. That will normally be a question for engineering evidence.

Conclusion

Employers' liability will, despite the legislative changes, remain a mainstay of personal injury litigation.

Firstly, unlike public liability claims, the presence of machinery and/or pathogens significantly increases the chances that any injury suffered will be significant. That means that, whilst such injuries are thankfully still rare, there is more reason to pursue a remedy should injury occur.

Secondly, whilst workplaces are undoubtedly safer than they were 50 or 100 years ago, there is an interesting corollary: as health and safety legislation, training and information have taken hold, common sense has been pushed to the side lines as people rely on express instruction rather than thinking for themselves. Absent adequate training, the scope for injury remains.

That shift in attitude is reflected in our lifestyles too. The incidence of back pain in men in their 20s is said to have increased by 25%[2] since the advent of the Manual Handling Operations Regulations 1992. We are more sedentary than 25 years ago, our posture is affected by our obsession with mobile technology, and we don't strengthen our backs with controlled lifting, unless we force ourselves into the weight-lifting section of the gym. If the workforce do not look after themselves, they are at ever increasing risk of harm if their employer does not take care.

Again, politics will come into play. To what extent do we want to protect the individual? That moral debate is for another place.

---

2   From 8% to 10%

PART FIVE

LIMITATION

CHAPTER TWELVE
THE LEGAL ISSUES

Should there be a time limit on bringing a claim for damages? On the face of it, it's a simple enough question, but it gives rise to a tension between allowing a claimant to seek redress for an alleged wrong on the one hand, and ensuring that people do not suddenly face historic claims which should have been brought years ago. Most jurisdictions have rules to cover this sort of situation and the answer will often depend on the type of claim being considered. A libel is something which offends in the here and now and needs to be resolved swiftly, whereas the use of land which might allow somebody to acquire possession of that land cannot simply arise overnight. There needs to be an extended limitation period to allow the original owner of the land to work out what is going on.

In personal injury law there are other issues which might arise. Whilst a person who falls in a pothole and breaks his ankle realises his plight straightaway, the person who inhales asbestos might not realise that he has been injured for many years. The child who is sexually assaulted may not be in a position to make the complaint there and then and may not realise that what is happening is wrong. The law has to balance the various factors that might arise, having particular regard to the fact that in personal injury claims there are a whole host of nuanced variables which need to be taken into consideration.

The relevant legislation is the Limitation Act 1980, which defines the relevant time limit for issuing proceedings in respect of any given cause of action. Given that we're talking about personal injury claims, the most relevant sections are sections 11, 14, and 33 but that does not mean that the other provisions might not become relevant.

Before looking at the provisions of the Act, it is worth bearing in mind that limitation is a potential defence to a claim, but not one that automatically applies. A defendant can choose not to take the point. In many cases, with a time period which is absolute, a defendant will gleefully accept the windfall which arises when a claimant fails to issue proceedings in time, but there are circumstances where the parties might agree to extend the limitation period if, for instance, they hope to resolve the matter without formal court proceedings. In personal injury actions, as will be seen below, the court has a discretion to extend the limitation period (or, more precisely, to disapply the relevant limitation period) and there may be no purpose to taking a point which will be lost before the court.

Section 2 of the 1980 Act provides that an action in tort should not be brought after the expiration of six years from the date on which the cause of action accrued. There are no extensions available to a claimant of that six year period. It is worth starting with section 2 because there will be occasions (e.g. a road traffic accident) when the events giving rise to a claim may or may not give rise to a specific claim for personal injury. If the claim is for vehicle damage only, the relevant period is six years.

It is important to remember that the time period being discussed runs from the accrual of the cause of action. A child cannot sue in his own name and requires a litigation friend (a responsible adult, normally a parent, who can make decisions about the litigation on his behalf). Only when the child reaches the age of 18, and attains majority, does time start to run for the purposes of the litigation. This idea extends to a party who lacks capacity, whether as a result of an accident or otherwise, and cannot bring an action in his own right.

Section 11

Section 11 of the Act provides a special time limit for actions in respect of personal injuries and applies to any action whether in negligence, nuisance or breach of duty (whether under contract, statute or otherwise) where damages claimed consist of or include damages in respect of personal injuries to the claimant or any other person. The relevant period is one of three years either from the date on which the cause of action accrued or, if later, the date of knowledge of the person injured. If the person injured dies before that three year period expires then the three year period for bringing a claim on behalf of the estate starts to run from the date of death or the date of the personal representative's knowledge, whichever is later. In simple terms, if a person is injured, they have three years from the date of the injury to formally start a court case for damages and if they do not do so in time they are "time-barred".

Things are not, however, necessarily that simple. If one falls in a pothole, or gets hit by a car, there is an (almost) immediate awareness of the accident and that it has had an effect, but what about the worker who is exposed to a pathogen, such as asbestos, or a risk which accrues over time, such as a repetitive strain injury? He might be aware of the exposure, but is he aware of the effects? Section 11 of the Act addresses this issue, by introducing the concept of date of knowledge, and section 14 provides the definition in that regard.

Section 14

"Knowledge" for the purposes of the Act, requires an understanding that (a) the injury in question was significant; and (b) that the injury was attributable in whole *or in part* to the act or omission which is alleged to constitute negligence, nuisance or breach of duty (emphasis added); and (c) the identity of the defendant; and (d) if it is alleged that the act or omission was that of a person other than the defendant, the identity of that person and the additional facts supporting the bringing of the action against the defendant. Knowledge that any acts or omissions did or did not, as a matter of law, involve negligence, nuisance or breach of duty is irrelevant.

In terms of whether an injury is significant, the question (*per* section 14(2)) is whether the person whose date of knowledge is in question would reasonably have considered it sufficiently serious to justify his instituting proceedings for damages against a defendant who did not dispute liability and was able to satisfy a judgment. The requirement of reasonableness means that there is an objective test here: would a reasonable person, with the claimant's knowledge, conclude that there was something amiss? The remainder of the requirement is to remove the pitfalls of litigation from the equation.

Section 14(3) explains that a person's knowledge includes knowledge which he might reasonably have been expected to acquire (a) from facts observable or ascertainable by him; or (b) from facts ascertainable by him with the help of medical or other appropriate expert advice which it is reasonable for him to seek; but a person shall not be fixed under this subsection with knowledge of facts ascertainable only with the help of expert advice so long as he has taken all reasonable steps to obtain and, where appropriate, to act on, that advice.

In real terms, the first question is whether the reasonable layman would realise that there was a problem or that he should seek appropriate advice to investigate whether there was a problem. If he goes to his doctor and is told that there is nothing wrong with him he is unlikely to "know" that there is a problem which requires him to take legal action. Only when he has acquired the requisite knowledge does time start to run.

Section 33

What happens if a claimant misses the boat and fails to bring proceedings within the three-year period? This can be particularly difficult where there is a date of knowledge issue where the precise date on which time starts to run is unclear. Section 33 of the Act allows for the possibility that a claimant who misses the original three-year deadline can nevertheless bring his claim for damages.

Of course, because limitation is no more than a defence to a claim, a defendant might choose not to take a point if the claimant misses the deadline (and the parties might even agree to extend the deadline in advance), but where the claimant is, on the face of the matter, out of time he can apply to the court, asking for an order disapplying the provisions of section 11. This does not change his date of knowledge, or extend the time for bringing an action indefinitely, but allows the court to do justice in this situation that has arisen. It is this idea of justice and what is equitable which governs the court's approach and the starting point is section 33 of the Act.

The court has to balance the interests of the claimant, who potentially loses his right to claim compensation for his injuries on a technicality rather than on merit, with the interests of the defendant, who is entitled to a fair trial and who should not have to meet stale claims. If the court allows a claim to proceed, that can cause prejudice to a defendant. If the claimant is debarred from bringing his claim, that is a prejudice which he will suffer. It is a question of discretion in any given case.

Section 33(3) makes clear that the court needs to have regard to all the circumstances of the case, but sets out specific issues to be considered. The length of the delay is obviously material. If the claimant has missed the deadline by a day, it is hard to see what detriment the defendant might suffer. The real question is the extent to which the delay affects the cogency of the evidence which either party might wish to deploy in the case. If there is a significant delay in bringing proceedings, such that witnesses have died, or contact with those witnesses has been lost, or even if their memory of events is likely to have been significantly affected, these are good reasons why the section 33 discretion should not be exercised. How can it be fair to proceed with a trial where the witnesses who would have been called had the claim been brought within three years can no longer give evidence? It may be that there are contemporaneous records which allow the court to deal with issues fairly, but the longer the delay, the more likely it is that prejudice will arise and the court's sympathy for the claimant will be lessened.

The court will also have regard to the conduct of the defendant after the cause of action arose, particularly whether he responded to requests for information or inspection which might be pertinent to the claimant's claim. The defendant cannot simply stonewall a claimant and expect the court to bar the claimant from bringing his claim out of time.

The court can also have regard to the duration of any disability of the claimant arising after the date of the accrual of the cause of action, the extent to which he acted promptly once he knew that he might have a cause of action and the steps that he took to obtain medical, legal or other expert advice, together with the nature of any advice that he received.

Ultimately, the question is one of whether a fair trial is still possible, or whether that trial has been prejudiced by the delay caused by not issuing proceedings within the requisite time period. It may, of course, be the case that the court cannot accurately assess the degree of prejudice but may simply be driven to the conclusion that there is some prejudice which arises. A good example would be the case where the file of papers had been lost. It may be that the parties are able to reconstruct a file of papers and may be able to produce relevant documents that it is unlikely that the full file of papers can be reconstructed with accuracy and documents which could affect a party's case either positively or negatively may now be missing, even if neither party is aware that such a document might have existed.

Over the years, the judicial sympathy towards claimants, stemming in the main from the Court of Appeal, has shifted slightly. Whilst once it seemed to be the case that as long as a fair trial was possible the claimant would be permitted to proceed, the current guidance tends to the view that the claimant is seeking an indulgence and that the onus is still on the claimant to persuade the court to hear his claim out of time.

CHAPTER THIRTEEN
THE FACTUAL ISSUES

Against that legal background, the practitioner actually has a fairly simple task, albeit that he will need to work through the various stages methodically. The first question is in identifying the point in time when time starts to run. Is this a straightforward accident where there is no issue about that date? Is there a delay in time start to run because the claimant is a child or otherwise under disability? If not then the starting point is clear.

If, however, this is a date of knowledge case, what facts and matters are material to the claimant forming the opinion that he might have a claim? A good example of the problems that arise would be a claim for noise induced hearing loss where the claimant, perhaps now in late middle age, worked many years ago in a noisy environment. Over time, he becomes aware that his hearing is not particularly good. Is that because he's getting older? Is part of his hearing loss down to the exposure to excessive noise? How can he tell the difference? What prompts him to take action? If he seeks medical assistance of his own accord, it is probably because he has come to the realisation that he has a problem that needs resolving, or at least addressing. If he seeks assistance because somebody tells him that he can claim compensation for being deaf, the reality is that he has already come to appreciate that he has a problem, but simply hasn't done anything about it. Just because he has not taken action does not mean that time has not already started to run.

The position can also be affected by the extent of the injury. If the damage to his hearing is very modest, he is unlikely to appreciate that the injury stems from his work environment. If on the other hand he has significant deafness at a young age then, objectively, one must question any assertion that he was unaware of the problem or the fact that, having worked in a noisy environment for many years, that may have caused or contributed to it. Simply asserting that a claimant was aware of a problem with his hearing 12 months or so before seeking medical or legal advice is a dangerous game. The onset of deafness is almost inevitably gradual and when analysed closely the complaint, for instance, that the volume on the television is now higher than it used to be will often transpire to reveal a steady increase in volume level over many many years.

The practical difficulty is that the claimant who is unrealistic in his assertion of a late date of knowledge is less likely to elicit the sympathy of the court when he asks for the exercise of its discretion under section 33 once he is found to be time-barred.

The second issue is the relevant time period. Is there any reason why the standard three years should not be the applicable timescale? For the reasons set out above that is unlikely to change although there are scenarios where short time periods may apply if, for instance, the accident occurs on an aeroplane.

If, and only if, the claim form is delivered to court after the expiry of limitation period does one need to consider the provisions of section 33. This is important because, for instance, one claimant might be out of time but his co-claimant, under the age of 18 at the time of the accident, may still be within time. The first claimant is time-barred, the second is not. It may be that the evidential position has changed in the period since the first claimant was time-barred such that, if his action was considered in isolation, he would be unable to overcome the hurdle of prejudice, but if the second claimant, bringing his action in time, faces the same prejudice, such that the court would still have to reach a conclusion on the same suboptimal evidence, can it be said that it is equitable to debar the first claimant? The court still has to make a decision, and it does not sit easily that, looking at the same evidence and asking the same question in respect of the first claimant and the second claimant, the court could only find in favour of the latter because apparent holes in the evidence gave rise to prejudice for the purposes of section 33 application. Ultimately, the question is probably a fact sensitive one, but the situation can and does arise.

The simplest approach is to go through the various factors set out in section 33(3), considering the factual elements of each in turn. What is the delay? Why did it happen? What is the effect of that delay? The layman should be able to identify the answer to those questions. Admittedly, there may be circumstances where the need for expert advice from, for instance, a medical practitioner, might play a part, but the simpler the analysis, the more compelling it is likely to be. If one or other party can explain to the court, in simple terms, why a fair trial can or cannot go ahead, the court is likely to be persuaded to that point of view. Accordingly, questions such as "What evidence was or would have been available at the time?", "What evidence is available now?" and "What evidence has been lost?" should be asked and addressed at the outset.

The question then arises as to whether the limitation issue should be dealt with as a preliminary matter, with a separate trial date and witnesses giving evidence solely on that point, or whether the whole question is so wrapped up with the factual matrix of the claim that the matter should be determined at trial. Defendants often take a limitation point, particularly in disease type cases, as a tactical step with a view to putting pressure on a claimant not to proceed, but do not wish to incur the expense of a separate trial when, on balance, the limitation point is not the strongest argument. From a claimant's perspective, early resolution of the limitation issue, removing that uncertainty from the equation, whilst it might compromise the entire claim, is normally a sensible idea: whilst he might lose, a split trial on the question of limitation may well speed up the resolution of his claim and will remove any uncertainty in that regard. Equally, the defendant, faced with a split trial, has to decide whether the point has sufficient merit to run it to a hearing, or whether this is one of those cases where it will take the point as a matter of policy to discourage such claims being brought.

Whole books have been written on the question of limitation in personal injury actions. There is a significant volume of case law on the points. Whilst the exercise of the section 33 discretion is a fact sensitive one, the vast majority of scenarios have been dealt with before. If such an argument arises, a more detailed consideration of the cases will be required to gain the necessary guidance as to whether the point has merit.

PART SIX

QUANTUM ISSUES

CHAPTER FOURTEEN
GENERAL DAMAGES

In general terms, there are two types of compensation. The simplest is direct compensation for financial losses arising from the injuries suffered. These are known as "special damages". The second, slightly more complicated, type of compensation is where the money awarded is said to compensate for non-financial losses such as the injury itself or the effects of such an injury on the claimant's lifestyle which cannot simply be overcome by incurring an additional expense. These are known as "general damages". General damages normally take the form of an apparently arbitrary award (subject to existing guidance) rather than a calculated figure.

There is an interesting question as to whether future financial loss falls to be considered as general damages or special damages. Technically, because the award is designed to reflect something that has not yet occurred, future financial losses are general damages but in practice they are normally dealt with as special damages because they are at least heads of claim where the loss is a financial one. That is not to say that the fairest way to deal with certain types of future loss is not, in any event, an award of general damages.

It is normally helpful to consider the question of general damages first because determining the physical or psychological effects of an injury on the claimant will influence how one approaches the calculation of financial loss. This chapter deals with two of the most commonly seen claims for general damages: pain, suffering and loss of amenity, and loss of congenial employment.

Pain, Suffering and Loss of Amenity

It is fairly trite that a genuinely injured party would rather not have been injured (and thus not qualify for compensation) than receive a cheque. Money will not stop his ongoing symptoms, or cause his amputated finger to regrow. Originally, judges would assess the appropriate award based on their experience and previous, similar, cases which were drawn to their attention, but in 1992 the Judicial Studies Board (as it then was) published a set of guidelines, setting out a variety of different types of injury and a range of suitable awards in each case. The purpose was to increase certainty by introducing a uniformity to the basis for the assessment of such awards. Practitioners would still cite previously reported cases, either to reinforce the suggestion that a particular bracket was applicable or to highlight the appropriate award within the bracket.

Of course, such awards are subject to inflationary pressures and therefore tend to increase over time. A second edition followed, and by 2013, when the Judicial Studies Board changed its name to the Judicial College, the 12th edition had been published. At the time of writing, the 14th edition is current. The format has not changed significantly, although death is now acknowledged to be a form of personal injury, warranting the first chapter. Certain brackets now contain significantly more information and guidance than originally. Minor injuries now have their own section.

In the case of a discrete injury, the starting point is therefore to identify the appropriate bracket, cross-referencing the medical evidence available, the claimant's account of how he has been affected, and the guidelines themselves and then determine where within that bracket the appropriate figure lies. There is rarely an absolute figure. Each case has the potential to differ.

The situation is made more complicated where a claimant sustains injury to more than one part of the body. He is entitled to one award for the totality of his injuries and therefore one has to look at the awards which might apply to any given injury in isolation but then factor in the overlap between those awards, the total period over which the claimant is affected by the injuries, the need for surgery, medication or other treatment, and the effects on that particular claimant. One does not simply add the figures together. The fracture of both fourth and fifth fingers on the same hand is unlikely to give an award significantly in excess of that for a fracture to the forefinger alone, whilst the loss of sight in both eyes is clearly of far more significant value than twice the loss of one eye. Again, each case falls to be determined on its merits.

There are still published cases upon which one can rely. Most sources now update the appropriate award for inflation and the like. One needs to bear in mind that the advocate who reports a case most likely does so because he achieved a good result for whichever side he was representing, and with experience comes knowledge that particular judges or particular courts might represent outliers when it comes to the validity of the awards made. Nevertheless, particularly in unusual cases or those where the brackets are not well defined, reported cases remain a useful tool to persuade the court as to the appropriate award.

As novices, all lawyers try to adopt a mechanical approach to the assessment of general damages: after all, how difficult can it be? One month of whiplash gets a claimant £X, two months gives rise to an award of £Y and so on, but one claimant might require strong painkillers and physiotherapy to make that recovery whilst another might carry on as normal with occasional twinges. A cogent description from the claimant as to the effects of the injury can influence the award made by the judge. Whilst such injuries are required to be supported and evidenced by medical reports, those reports are often produced in standard form with little or no detail as to the reality of the situation. The key is to talk to the claimant to see how they have actually been affected.

That is not to say that the court will ignore the guidelines, but rather that within any given bracket there is normally some scope for manoeuvre. Certain injuries can be particularly subjective. Scarring is the classic example. The guidelines award significantly greater sums to female claimants than would be awarded to a man for the same injury, although whether such discrimination can survive in the longer term is open to doubt. As an interesting corollary, the writer once represented a severely disabled claimant who had suffered nasty lacerations to both knees which had left significant scars. The suggestion that the claimant, who could not demonstrate any awareness of her scarring or its physical effect, should receive a lesser award than might have objectively been justified for such injuries was met with very short shrift by the district judge who had to approve settlement.

The award of general damages is designed to reflect not just the claimant's pain and suffering, but also their loss of amenity. The original idea was that whilst one individual might suffer more pain than the next, his capacity to deal with it might be greater such that the two factors might balance out and the loss of amenity, the day-to-day effect of the injury, might be the same. However, there are other types of loss of amenity. Some of those can be overcome by financial compensation in the form of special damages: the keen golfer with a foot injury might claim the cost of hiring a golf cart each and every time he plays so that he does not have to struggle to walk around the course. Some hobbies, equally consuming, are not so easy to replicate or facilitate with financial compensation. The keen horseman who can no longer ride because of back pain cannot simply spend money to remedy that issue. Technically, the award for loss of amenity is designed to cover that, but the reality is that for the claimant who can no longer engage in his previously all-consuming hobby the award, any award, will not compensate him for that loss. Indeed, the awards made are often almost insulting to somebody who feels that strongly about what they used to be able to do.

For those reasons it is often worth investigating whether there are alternative ways in which the injured party might continue their previous lifestyle or at least come close to it, but the courts tend not to be overly generous in that regard.

Loss of Congenial Employment

The other commonly seen claim for general damages is award for loss of congenial employment. The idea here is that certain types of employment offer a worker an additional level of gratification, above and beyond the financial remuneration available such that the effect of losing that employment as a result of injury is not just a loss of money but a loss of enjoyment, of lifestyle, of the claimant's sense of self. Policemen, firemen, paramedics, members of the Armed Forces and the like often put forward the argument that their job involves adrenaline, unusual activities, altruism and/or a sense of self-worth which means that an additional award is appropriate when they then have to take a less exciting role. The awards made tend to be relatively modest, a few thousand pounds, but there is a difficult argument here: Who is to determine whether any particular form of employment is more worthy than the next? A shop worker may revel in the day-to-day human contact that such a role provides. The lawyer may feel that no other role would give the same satisfaction. Each might equally feel that the job is nothing more than that: a job, undertaken solely for monetary award. If one is to compensate the individual claimant for being deprived of a specific type of employment (rather than their earnings), where does that end? A claimant may say, "I really enjoyed the job that I was doing with X Co. but I lost that job as a result of the accident. I am now working in the same role with Y Co. but I don't enjoy it in the same way because the people are different." The loss of amenity is there, but it is highly unlikely to sound in damages.

For the purposes of this book it suffices to say that claims for loss of congenial employment can be made but that they are limited in their extent and value and will depend on the facts of the case.

CHAPTER FIFTEEN
SPECIAL DAMAGES:
PAST LOSSES

As set out in the previous chapter, most claims involve some sort of financial loss. This could be as trivial as the cost of painkillers or a wasted bus fare but in most cases special damages represent if not the majority of the claim then at least a significant proportion of the claim for compensation. Some of those costs will already have been incurred. Some may only occur in the future. Sometimes there will be an ongoing loss which will continue either for a defined period or for the rest of the claimant's life. Most of these losses are fairly obvious but the purpose of a claim for compensation is to put the claimant back in the position they would have been in had the accident not occurred and that can involve some lateral thinking to ensure that all potential losses are compensated.

With that in mind it is worth considering the standard heads of claim that one habitually sees. Obviously not all heads of loss appear in all claims but the same building blocks need to be considered in each case. This chapter deals with the heads of loss most commonly incurred in the immediate aftermath of an accident whilst the next chapter deals with future losses.

Property damage

Perhaps the simplest claims are those for property damaged in the accident. That might be the car that the claimant was driving, clothes damaged by being ripped, bloodied, or being cut from the claimant's body by the emergency services, or personal effects which are damaged in the accident. The claimant is entitled to be put back in the position that he would have been in the accident not occurred. In some cases that is easily achieved: if he is wearing a new pair of jeans which are damaged beyond repair, he is entitled to the cost of replacement jeans. If his iPhone is smashed, he is entitled to a replacement.

The difficulty arises when the object damaged is not new. In the case of cars there is a significant second-hand market which means that one can value the damaged vehicle with reasonable accuracy although even then a special edition vehicle might have some sort of special interest value because no like for like replacement is available. What normally happens is that an assessor inspects the vehicle, considers its pre-accident state in terms of any damage and the mileage on the vehicle, both of which are acknowledged to affect the value and then reaches a view as to the likely pre-accident value, considers the salvage value and opines that the claimant's loss is the difference between the two. The claimant may challenge that, particularly if there are unique aspects to the damaged vehicle, but the process is fairly clear-cut.

The same cannot be said of other second-hand objects. A heavily worn pair of jeans, a ripped T-shirt and scuffed trainers have little intrinsic value and the reality is that the claimant will have to buy a new outfit. Often the offer made will be a proportion of the replacement cost on the basis that the claimant has already had some benefit from the items previously purchased and will be better off when he replaces them.

Medical Treatment costs

The next most likely head of loss is the cost of medical treatment. This can range from painkillers and visiting the GP, through physiotherapy and other conservative treatment options, to surgical intervention. Often this treatment is provided by the NHS and the hospital charges incurred fall to be repaid by a compensator when a claimant is registered. Those costs are payable in addition to the claim.

If the claimant has paid privately for his treatment to date then, as long as he can prove causation and that the losses were reasonably incurred, he is entitled to reclaim those costs from the defendant. Whilst strictly speaking it should be considered in the next chapter, a claimant is normally entitled to claim the cost of future medical treatment on a privately paid basis. The logic is that he should not be subject to waiting times or restrictions on his treatment options by being stuck in the NHS and should therefore be put in funds to allow him to seek treatment on a private basis. That said, if the treatment is inevitably available on the NHS (e.g. particular types of surgery or the provision of hearing aids) then the claimant may not be in a position to recover those costs.

Aids and Appliances

The effect of an accident may mean that the claimant incurs costs in buying equipment to make life simpler. He may need to buy or hire a wheelchair if he is in plaster and cannot walk. He may need to install a second banister to allow him to go up and down stairs safely. Somebody with a hand injury may require a mechanical can opener, and one often sees claims for robotic vacuum cleaners and even full body hot air dryers (particularly useful for those with shoulder injuries which prevent them from drying their backs after a shower). For more significant modifications to the home with, perhaps, the installation of a downstairs toilet, a wet room bathroom, or a more usable kitchen if the injuries are serious and are likely to be long-standing. The claim is normally for the base cost of the equipment with an allowance made for regular replacement in the future, to be assessed using the principles set out in the next chapter.

Care and Assistance

Above and beyond the use of equipment after an accident, a claimant may require care and assistance. Sometimes this is provided on a commercial basis, in which case it is normally a simple task to present the relevant invoices and reclaim that cost. More commonly, that care is provided by a family member or friend. That is not normally a commercial arrangement but the courts recognise that such care and assistance is capable of sounding in damages.

Not all care attracts compensation: making a cup of tea and proffering sympathy for a claimant's situation does not entitle that person to claim. Such claims are only valid in respect of care which goes well beyond the call of duty[1] and which would not be provided in any event. There is no lower limit to such claims[2] – they are not reserved for the

---

1 *Mills v British Rail Engineering Limited* [1992] 1 PIQR Q130

most serious of cases, but that does not mean that such compensation can be claimed in each and every case.

Clearly there is a spectrum: changing dressings, providing physical assistance in moving around the house, bathing people and the like will fall to be compensated. Tasks such as cleaning, cooking, and washing are fact dependent. Much will depend on who did the tasks before the accident and the extent of the likely claim. If a spouse is providing assistance with domestic tasks which benefit the rest of the family (as such tasks will normally do), it is much harder to persuade a court that (a) they go well beyond the call of duty; (b) they would not have been performed in any event; and/or (c) they should sound in damages.

In assessing the value of the care provided, the starting point is normally an appropriate commercial rate for the provision of such care, less a discount[3] to reflect the fact that neither National Insurance nor Income Tax is payable on such an award (whether a settlement, or court awarded figure). There are occasional arguments about whether the commercial rate should be a composite rate (i.e. one that acknowledges that care might be provided throughout the day and night and at weekends) or a more standard daytime rate. Ultimately, because the care is rarely provided for an exact period of time on an exact day of the week, such claims are more of an educated guess than a definitive calculation.

Services

On top of the traditional personal care and assistance claims, one often sees a claim for the cost of employing professionals to undertake those tasks which, but for the accident, the claimant would have undertaken. Gardening, ironing, domestic cleaning, decorating (labour only – you can't claim for expensive wallpaper!) are all areas where more seriously injured claimants might seek assistance. As with traditional care claims, the issues are whether the claimant would have obtained that assistance in any event, and whether that assistance is provided by a professional

---

2 *Giambrone v Sun World Holidays Limited* [2004] EWCA Civ 158 where the Court of Appeal upheld modest care awards in the context of parents looking after children with gastroenteritis.

3 *Housecroft v Burnett* [1986] 1 All ER 332

(in which case the whole cost would be the sum payable) or on a gratuitous basis (in which case the *Housecroft* discount would apply). Claimants normally obtain quotes from local tradesmen, setting out how long such tasks would take, the likely cost, and the frequency with which the work would fall to be done. The medical evidence needs to dovetail with the claims brought, identifying how the injury prevents the claimant from undertaking that activity, or at least makes it reasonable to buy in that assistance.

In serious cases, the parties will often obtain expert care evidence, identifying the claimant's requirements and the likely cost of providing that care and assistance. Such reports often extend to cover the costs of rehabilitation, together with suitable aids and appliances. Again, that evidence needs to be based on the medical evidence in the first instance.

Interest

Finally in this section, it is worth noting that a successful claimant is normally entitled to interest on those losses which have gone uncompensated since they were incurred. He needs to plead the claim under section 69 of the County Courts Act 1984, and is normally entitled to 2%pa on general damages from the date of service of proceedings, the full special account rate (currently 0.5%pa!) on losses sustained in the immediate aftermath of the accident and at half the full special account rate (i.e. 0.25%pa) on ongoing losses (e.g. his loss of earnings or care). Suffice to say that this is included for the sake of completion, rather than financial value.

CHAPTER SIXTEEN
SPECIAL DAMAGES: FUTURE LOSSES

The purpose of an award for compensation is to put the claimant back in the position that he would have been in had the accident not happened and that is quite straightforward when the loss has already been incurred. If I have had to spend £100 on medical treatment as a result of the accident then it is a simple task to reclaim that sum. The more difficult scenario is trying to work out what will happen in the future when the effects of the accident are ongoing. How much money does the claimant need now to make sure that he is not out of pocket in the future but equally is not overcompensated?

Historically, courts would make awards of general damages for future loss, not least because there was no easy mathematical methodology available to be more accurate. However, with the advent of actuarial understanding and commonly available statistics and actuarial tables, courts have felt far more comfortable in adopting a more scientific approach.

Multiplier/Multiplicands

In *Wells v Wells*[1] the House of Lords was asked to determine the correct method of calculating lump sum damages for the loss of future earnings and the costs of future care.

The principle is relatively straightforward: if one imagines a money/time graph with time on the x axis and money on the y axis, giving a claimant a set amount of money now, which will be spent at a steady rate over time (which represents, for instance, a loss of salary), gives rise to a straight line reduction in the fund until the money has been spent. Of course, if one invests the money over that period, the fund falls to be topped up with interest from time to time, so that in theory the fund will last longer. That means that in reality one might not need as much money now to last the requisite period of time.

---

1 [1999] 1 AC 345

That analysis does not take into account inflation. A claimant might reasonably expect his salary to increase over time to reflect the general increase in the cost of living. In the normal course of events that would cause the fund to reduce increasingly quickly over time. Moreover, nobody can say with any certainty what the rate of inflation will be at any given point in time. The remedy to this problem is to assess the effect of interest by reference to the underlying rate of inflation so that when one assesses how much interest will be paid into the fund by way of top up, the calculation is based on the net interest (i.e. after tax) relative to inflation, whatever the prevailing rate of inflation is at that point in time. That way, one adds in, and then subtracts, inflation so the calculation becomes inflation neutral. This net interest rate is known as the 'discount rate'. The court in *Wells* was asked how that discount rate should be determined and at what level.

Back in the 1990s, there were significant arguments as to what the appropriate discount rate should be. Interest rates and inflation were high, and rates of return were relatively generous. In *Wells* the court decided that the appropriate rate should be 3%[2]. This meant that it was relatively easy to calculate the appropriate lump sum. Pre-calculated actuarial tables, drawn up by (and named after) the then government actuary Sir Michael Ogden were published. There were separate tables for losses to (and from) specific ages (50, 55, 60, 65, 70, 75) together with life tables (i.e. the sum required to compensate a claimant for their remaining life expectancy) and each table was calculated separately for men and women, the latter having the longer life expectancy.

To calculate the appropriate loss of earnings for a man to a retirement age of, say, 65, one would turn up the appropriate table, identify the relevant column (by reference to the discount rate) and then find the appropriate figure in that column for a man of the claimant's current age, interpolating between the two birthdays as appropriate. This figure is known as the multiplier.

---

2 Based on evidence that the prudent investor would invest in Index Linked Government Stocks which, whilst not giving the same rate of return as other investments, were less at risk of the vagaries of the stock market, because they provided specific rates of return.

CHAPTER SIXTEEN – SPECIAL DAMAGES: FUTURE LOSSES: THE THEORY

One would then calculate the annual net loss of earnings at current rates (because there is no tax payable on damages) which figure is known as the multiplicand. Multiplying the multiplicand by the multiplier would give the loss of earnings figure. If appropriate, one would subtract any residual earning capacity.

In 2001, the then Lord Chancellor, Lord Irvine of Lairg, issued a statement, setting a discount rate of 2.5%. The lower the discount rate, the less the fund will be topped up by the interest received, so the fund needs to be correspondingly greater at the start of the process. The basis of that decision was simply that rates of return had reduced and the suggestion from 1999 that 3%pa was appropriate could not be sustained.

Since 2001 there have been a number of attempts by claimants to persuade successive Lords Chancellor to reconsider the discount rate but it has remained at 2½%, even in the face of the threat of judicial review. However, on 27 February 2017, the Lord Chancellor, Liz Truss made an announcement (interestingly via the London Stock Exchange) that she was changing the discount rate and reducing it to -0.75%. The fact that the change was so great is, perhaps, evidence of its overdue nature, but the effect has been seismic.

To give an example, the appropriate multiplier for a 40-year-old man to retirement at state retirement age (67) was, at 2½%, 19.04, but is now, at -0.75%, 28.72. For a 20-year-old man to age 68, 27.48 has increased to 55.81. The new rate acknowledges that those investing in government stock cannot expect their investment to keep up with inflation. Rather than interest topping up the fund each year, the effect of inflation is to reduce the value of the investment even allowing for investment return. The effect has been so significant that the very methodology to be used in calculating the discount rate now falls to be reconsidered. New Ogden tables using the -0.75% rate have been published and circulated, and the profession is coming to terms with a significant increase in the value of claims for future loss.

From a defendant's perspective, a negative discount rate makes the possibility of a Periodical Payments Order (see Chapter 18) more attractive (perhaps for the first time) not least because with the funds available to an insurance company different investment strategies will allow them return in excess of the suggested discount rate. From a claimant's perspective such a resolution gives certainty, albeit for what would probably be a lesser capital value. The rule of three for claimants still applies.

Loss of Earnings

The multiplier/multiplicand approach can be applied to all heads of future loss, but is most commonly seen in the context of a loss of earnings claim. However, the original approach to such calculations (set out above) has been finessed to take into account a claimant's employability over the period to retirement. Research suggests that an individual's employability is dependent on a number of factors: gender, age, whether one is already employed[3], whether one is disabled or not[4], and the level of one's education will all influence the extent to which a claimant is likely to be or remain employed. Whilst the educational level makes little difference to the non-disabled, employed individual, the reality is that when one is rendered disabled and unemployed, poor academic qualifications render that person almost unemployable.

The calculation therefore normally takes the form of the pre-accident net earnings multiplied by the appropriate multiplier to the date when the claimant would have retired multiplied by the appropriate contingency as was in place before the accident (which gives the likely future earnings to retirement) less an equivalent calculation for the post-accident (i.e. current) position. The latter part of the calculation might see the claimant earning less money (e.g. because he can work part-time), retiring earlier (because of the effects of his injuries) and with a significantly reduced contingency. Interestingly, but perhaps obviously, for people close to retirement, being rendered unemployed normally has a significantly greater effect than being rendered disabled: if one is within six months of retirement, the chances of returning to the open labour market and/or then getting a job are very low.

---

3 Because it is easier to get a job if one already has a job.

4 Within the definition provided by the Disability Discrimination Act 1995, which requires a substantial, long-term disability which affects one's capacity for work.

For obvious reasons, this Ogden approach to future loss of earnings calculations tends to give rise to significantly higher awards than the old method: each of the three constituent parts to the post-accident calculation will potentially reduce giving a significant composite effect. The courts, wary of overcompensating claimants, often consider the extent of the disability contended for and modify the published contingencies accordingly. Nevertheless, with the discount rate reduction, any sort of Ogden-style calculation will, almost inevitably, give rise to a sizeable award.

Smith v Manchester

There are limitations to the Ogden approach. The classic situation is where a claimant, in full employment before the accident, suffers an injury which would compromise him were he to find himself on the open labour market but which does not prevent him from doing his current job. The injury itself may not be sufficient to render him disabled for the purposes of the Equality Act. He is still earning, as at trial, what he would have been earning had he not been injured. The Ogden calculation would potentially give rise to a nil loss.

The courts have dealt with this problem for many years by making lump sum awards of general damages to represent a claimant's disability on the open labour market. These awards are known as *Smith v Manchester* awards after the 1974 case of that name. The award made is commonly referenced to the claimant's earning capacity, with the relevant period being determined after consideration of the claimant's age, the likelihood of the claimant finding themselves on the open labour market and the extent of the disability posed by their injuries. Those awards have traditionally been very modest.

Importantly, there needs to be proper evidence dealing with the relevant points.

Blamire

The other circumstance where an award of general damages might be appropriate in a future loss claim scenario is where the claimant asserts that but for the accident they would have achieved a qualification or level of employment which is no longer available to them. The most well-known case of this nature is that of *Blamire*[5] where the court accepted that the claimant had lost the chance of a well-paid career but was unable to assess either the prospect of achieving the suggested professional goals or the likely remuneration which the claimant might have achieved. Again, as in the case of a *Smith* award, a broad brush lump sum approach is appropriate.

In certain circumstances a claimant might be able to claim two or even all three of the above types of award. There may be an ongoing loss of earnings which has already coalesced at the time of trial such that an Ogden calculation is the starting point but there remains the risk that were the claimant to lose their new employment they would be significantly disadvantaged on the open labour market. Moreover, their pre-accident chances of career development, which might have seen a significant salary increase had they come to fruition, may now lie in tatters. There is no reason in principle why the claimant should not receive a basic loss of earnings award calculated by reference to the Ogden calculation, a lump sum *Smith* award predicated on the existing and ongoing disability on the open labour market, and a separate *Blamire* award reflecting the lost opportunity.

From the practitioner's point of view, the trick is simply to stop and think. What might have happened had this accident not occurred? What can we prove? What are the prospects of such events coming to pass? What is the current situation? How will that affect the claimant? Simply breaking down the analysis into those relatively easy questions (even if the answers are not in fact obvious) should allow one to identify the appropriate way forward. A Smith award is a potentially useful position when there is undeniably a problem but no immediately ascertainable loss of earnings.

Loss of Pension claims

These potentially warrant a chapter on their own, which is certainly beyond the scope of this book, but such claims should not be ignored.

---

5 *Blamire v South Cumbria Health Authority* [1993] PIQR Q1, CA

As final salary schemes (where the employee receives a pension equal to a fraction of their final salary dependent on the length of their service) disappear from the marketplace and are replaced by money purchase schemes (where an employer and the employee both contribute to a fund which is ultimately used by an annuity or the like) the calculations become easier. One might reasonably take the annual cost of replacing the employer's contribution as the multiplicand and apply a calculation similar to that for future loss of earnings.

Aids and Appliances, Future Care and Services

All of these heads of claim can be approached in the same way: calculate the appropriate annual multiplicand and apply the appropriate multiplier. Bear in mind that most people will require external assistance in due course in any event. Claiming the cost of painting the outside of the claimant's house for the rest of his life means that you are asserting that he would still be climbing the long ladders into his 90s. In the case of an event which will only happen, say, every five years, take an annual multiplicand of 20% of the likely cost.

In such cases it is always worth bearing in mind that the claimant may need to purchase the requisite equipment immediately such that there is a capital cost claimed as a partial replacement cost subject to appropriate multiplier. That multiplier needs to discount the first year because the equipment has already been bought.

Accommodation claims

In some cases, a claimant will require new accommodation because of their injuries. The rule in *Roberts v Johnstone*[6] allows the claimant to claim on the basis of an annual multiplicand of 2½% of the additional capital cost in purchasing the larger (and thus more expensive) property. That 2½% figure reflected the interest which it was deemed that the claimant would have received had he had those monies available to him to invest. In other words, it reflected the discount rate.

---

6 [1989] 1 QB 878

126 • AN INTRODUCTION TO PERSONAL INJURY LAW

For obvious reasons, a negative discount rate means that the traditional form of calculation is now dead: an injured claimant would have to give credit for the costs of buying the new property. Various alternatives fall to be considered, with perhaps the most obvious one being a different approach to the calculation of the multiplicand. One suggestion would be to use the difference between the annual costs of servicing the respective mortgages and applying a suitable multiplier. Alternatively, one might see insurers buying properties outright and allowing injured parties to live in them for a peppercorn rent. These are interesting, but sadly overly complex, questions which fall outwith the scope of this book.

My favourite Ogden table

Table 27 of the Ogden tables sets out discounting factors for terms certain or, in English, the factor to be applied in determining how much is required now to invest over time to give a specific sum at a point in the future when the need arises to spend those monies. The classic case is where an injured claimant will require an operation such as a knee replacement in 10 years' time at, say, £5,000 at today's value. When the discount rate was 2½% the appropriate 10 year factor was 0.7812, so one needed £3,906 now to release sufficient funds when necessary. The effect of the new discount rate is that one now needs more than the current cost of the operation to allow for that surgery in the future.

There is no substitution for getting hold of a copy of the Ogden tables and working through them. Care should, however, be taken: The 0% column in tables 1 and 2 (the respective life tables) potentially represents one's own life expectancy. What you do with that information is a matter for you. The writer identified the precise day on which he was officially 'over the hill' and threw a drinks party to mark it.

PART SEVEN

MISCELLANEOUS ISSUES

CHAPTER SEVENTEEN
THINGS WE NEED TO KNOW THAT WE DON'T NEED TO KNOW

This chapter deals, briefly, with things of which, at an introductory level, one only needs to be aware.

Interim payments

The claimant may find himself in financial difficulties as a result of his injuries. If he can show that he will recover substantial (rather than nominal) damages from a defendant, he can ask (or apply to the court) for an interim payment – a payment on account of his damages. He does not need to show need for that sum, although it can sway the judicial mind. He does, however, have to show that he is not receiving more than a reasonable proportion of his claim, as there still needs to be a balance to be paid to achieve settlement.

A defendant can make payments in respect of certain heads of loss (e.g. the value of the claimant's vehicle) or generally. In some cases, the interim actually relates to treatment or medical investigations which do not form part of the claim itself, and the parties need to be careful to keep clear records of what needs to be set off when final negotiations occur. On one occasion, the parties reached a settlement of £300,000, only for the defendant to assert that they had paid £1,000 more in interim payments than the claimant accepted that she had received. With the whole settlement about to unravel, it was pointed out that the difference had been used to pay for physiotherapy which had not formed part of the claimant's schedule and the matter was resolved.

If a claimant needs to force the issue of an interim payment, he will have to issue proceedings. This might force him into litigation earlier than he or the defendant would like, and with the advent of increased issue fees, that can cause other problems, but those, thankfully, are not for consideration here.

Provisional damages

In some cases, the claimant suffers an injury where his condition is currently stable, but there is a very small risk that, in the long-term, there will be a catastrophic deterioration in his condition. In those cases, he can potentially resolve his claim on the basis that his current condition will not deteriorate, but, unusually, reserves the right to come back for more compensation in the unlikely event that the deterioration comes to pass. Such an arrangement is known as a provisional damages award, because the original award is provisional on the claimant not deteriorating. The trigger for coming back to court needs to be closely defined.

In the majority of cases, a defendant would rather settle the case on a once and for all basis, paying off the risk at an early stage to achieve finality. That normally involves a rough calculation of the likely damages in the event that the deterioration comes to pass and then assessing that risk. From the claimant's point of view, such settlements are the epitome of the rule of three: Do I accept more damages now, to resolve the matter once and for all, but accept the risk that I might deteriorate significantly, or do I want the security of a provisional damages award? Such cases are obviously specialist and beyond the scope of this work.

Periodical Payments Orders

Damages are normally paid on a one-off basis, but the law allows (and in cases above a certain value requires) the parties to consider whether a periodical payment order (PPO) is appropriate. In these cases, where there is a need for, say, ongoing care or accommodation costs to be met, the parties can agree (or the court can order) that that part of the claimant's compensation is paid not on an up-front basis, but on a regular (normally annualised) basis.

That payment is normally increased on an index-linked basis, but ceases upon the claimant's death. That means that the money does not run out, but also means that if the claimant were to die unexpectedly early, the payments stop too, so the value of the claim is correspondingly diminished. Such agreements arguably represent a fair means to compensate a claimant, but they do restrict the claimant's right to do with the money as he pleases, as he only receives a relatively modest amount at any given time and it is normally earmarked for a specific purpose. Again, if the injury warrants a PPO, it is probably beyond the scope of this book.

The Compensation Recovery Unit

If a claimant receives state benefits as a result of his injuries, the question arises as to who should bear that cost. If, for instance, a claimant would have earned £10,000 during his absence from work, but receives £4,000 in benefits, he is only £6,000 out of pocket. Were the defendant to pay him £6,000, he would be back in the position that he would have been in, but the government has paid him £4,000 which it would not have had to but for the accident. The answer is that the Compensation Recovery Unit will reclaim that £4,000 at the conclusion of the litigation, so the claimant claims the full extent of his loss (£10,000) and gives credit for the benefits received. The defendant pays the £10,000, but pays £4,000 of that to the CRU and £6,000 to the claimant, so that the claimant gets his £10,000 (£4,000 in benefits, £6,000 in compensation), the government gets its £4,000 back, and the defendant pays the full amount.

If on the above example the claimant had contributed to his accident (say 25%), he would only be due 75% of his loss, so he would be able to claim £7,500, the defendant would have to pay that figure, the claimant would receive £3,500 and the £4,000 would still be repaid to the CRU.

Only certain benefits attract these provisions and each falls to be set off against the equivalent head of loss in the main claim. If there is no equivalent claim made by the claimant, the defendant still has to repay the benefits, but isn't allowed to set off the entirety of the benefits against the claim made.

Each case has to be registered with the CRU, and a party can apply for a Certificate of Recoverable Benefit (aka "a CRU certificate") which sets out the total benefits payable as at any given date (because the benefits are often ongoing), together with a breakdown of which benefits have been paid.

Importantly, particularly from the claimant's point of view, the conclusion of the case (or 5 years from the date of the accident if earlier) brings an end to the obligation to give credit for the benefits received. In other words, if a claimant is receiving benefits at the conclusion of the case, he will continue to receive those benefits, and does not have to repay any future benefits out of his damages.

If a defendant makes an interim payment, he will normally have to discharge the outstanding benefits as at that point in time.

Finally, a defendant can appeal the certificate at the conclusion of the case, by paying the outstanding balance, and then filing an appeal arguing that any benefits paid after a certain date were not paid as a result of the accident. The classic case is where the claimant is not, in fact, as injured as he would have people believe, or has an underlying condition which means that he would have required the benefits in any event.

Personal Injury Trusts

Some state benefits are means tested, and giving a claimant a substantial sum of money can have the effect of disqualifying the claimant from the state aid which he needs and to which he is entitled. The answer is to place the compensation monies in a personal injury trust, a mechanism set up by the government to avoid this problem. In effect, whilst the claimant has the benefit of the money, legal ownership of the money vests in a trustee, who is obliged to act in the claimant's best interests. The state cannot then take that money into account when considering what benefits are payable, but the claimant will have to ask the trustee to release money as and when needed. The claimant is, however, allowed to hold some money (currently some £16,000) in his own name without falling foul of the means-testing provisions.

Court Approval

As we saw in chapter 2, some people are not allowed to litigate without a litigation friend to look after their interests and make decisions on their behalf. The most common such category is children, who cannot make decisions until they reach 18. As a result, any proposed settlement must be put before the court for approval.

Proceedings are issued for that sole purpose, an Advice from counsel is obtained, setting out the range of opinion and the reasonableness of the settlement figure, theoretically adopting the claimant's rule of three. Those papers are put before the judge, normally in the presence of the child (whose identity needs to be proved with the birth certificate), with the judge confirming that the factual matrix is correct before approving the settlement. Until that settlement is approved, it is not final and either party can back out.

The same situation applies to cases where adult claimants lack capacity – until the court says the settlement is appropriate, either side can withdraw, meaning that negotiations in such cases are always subject to the proviso that the court must approve the agreed figure. If the court does not, the parties will be invited to resolve their differences, but if they cannot, the matter will be transferred to the normal litigation pathway and proceed to trial.

Investment of Awards

Historically, the Court Funds Office offered very favourable interest rates, which meant that litigants were keen to invest their money there, even to the point of claiming that they were younger than they were so that the money could accrue interest for longer (hence the requirement for the birth certificate!) but that is no longer the case, and alternative investments are permitted.

What should happen is that the award is invested until the claimant reaches 18, when the accrued sums are released to him. They cannot be withheld. However, it may be that the claimant has need of that money in the interim period. As long as the purpose is sufficiently educational or otherwise for the benefit of the child (e.g. computing, but not video gaming, equipment, school trips which could not otherwise be afforded), then the money can be drawn down as long as there remains a reasonably substantial sum for when the claimant reaches 18.

The situation is more difficult where the claimant is never going to gain his independence and will remain an assisted party, but the compensation is not in respect of his care requirements (e.g. because somebody who lacks capacity has met with a relatively modest accident). The fund will need to be spent for his benefit, but cannot just be released to him. One solution is to identify a regular holiday which the claimant might take and use the funds to permit him to enjoy that holiday each year until the money is exhausted.

CHAPTER EIGHTEEN
THINGS WE NEED TO KNOW, BUT PROBABLY DON'T WANT TO

There are things which we need to know, but which are simply beyond the scope of this book which has, by now, one hopes, reached the limits of the definition of its title. This chapter, then, is a conclusion or, perhaps, a dystopic denouement – a warning to the bright-eyed and enthusiastic personal injury lawyer in waiting.

Costs, The Past and The Future

Costs are the *raison d'être* of the personal injury lawyer, without which none of us would be able to operate. Sadly, the full history of the law of costs is too interesting and/or complex to warrant inclusion. Moreover, the law is in a constant state of flux. Suffice it to say that the traditional model was that the winner would be paid his costs by the loser, and in the case of the successful claimant, those costs would be recovered in addition to his damages.

Then, because some cases lost, it was decided that claimant lawyers would be paid a bonus on the cases they won, to make up for not getting paid on the cases that they lost. They were originally expected to take that bonus from their own client's damages, but that proved unworkable, because (a) clients wanted to keep all their damages; and (b) the damages weren't enough to allow the lawyers to take enough money to pay the uplift in any event.

Within a couple of years, the law changed so that the uplift was recoverable from the unsuccessful defendant. That had its injustices, in that one defendant might end up paying double in the case that he lost to reflect that had he won it, he wouldn't have paid anything. Nevertheless, the overall model was vaguely cost-neutral on both sides.

Sadly, the position is no longer so simple. The Jackson Reforms reversed the rules on the recoverability of uplifts, so that defendants don't have to pay extra if they lose, the corollary being that the claimant lawyer does not get paid at all if he loses, and does not get paid extra if he wins. There are nuances, with awards for injury being increased by 10%, supposedly as a sop to the fact that the solicitors now take a proportion of the damages to cover their uplift (not that the sums which they can take cover the likely uplift on counsel's fees).

Is there a future for personal injury law? The obsession of successive governments, and the insurance industry, is to drive down the cost of claims, either because one believes that the cost to society is too great, or because one subscribes to the need for insurers to be profitable. There is, of course, an irony, that people who cannot get their compensation from insurers fall to be looked after by the state, but that requires a degree of joined up thinking.

Various solutions have been brought forward, all of which have had significant effects on the claimant side of the profession. Some have already been mentioned, but it is worth reviewing the whole picture.

Firstly, there has been a drive towards reducing the costs recoverable by lawyers representing claimants with fixed fees being introduced, rarely representing the work required to do the job to a professional standard. This is a direct reflection of the claimant solicitors seeking to industrialise the process for their financial benefit. Faced with increasing numbers of claims, the defendants demanded that costs be reduced, which, in turn, required claimants to take more cases to make the same money, driving standards down to maintain profits.

Then the Legal Aid, Sentencing and Punishment of Offenders Act 2012 (LASPO), meant that for cases after March 2013, a claimant lawyer could not recover a success fee from the defendant in the event of a win. That means that lawyers, unlike pretty much any other profession[1], are expected to work without knowing if, when or how much they will be paid, with barristers in particular often having to bear their own travel expenses and the like, only to be at the whim of the court and their own clients, often without the chance to assess the client before the day of trial.

---

1 Another notable case is that of authors.

Accordingly, unless they can recover the uplift from their own client's damages (which are unlikely to release sufficient funds), they are now entitled to be paid the going rate if they win and nothing if they lose. The equivalent would be to ask a paramedic to work on the basis that he only gets paid if the patient survives not only his original involvement, but also more generally.

LASPO also introduced the concept of Qualified One-way Costs Shifting (QOCS) such that a successful claimant gets his costs, but the successful defendant cannot, unless it can be shown that the claimant has brought the claim dishonestly. The difficulty with that is that even now, 4 years on, lawyers, and particularly judges, whose only experience in practice was under the traditional "loser pays" system default to that position, when the reality is that it was supposed to bring in a completely new system of funding claims. Courts are increasingly looking for reasons to make an unsuccessful claimant pay the defendant's costs, even though that was not the intention.

The Enterprise and Regulatory Reform Act 2013 (see Chapter 10) then made it much more difficult for claimants injured at work to claim compensation, increasing uncertainty as to whether they would be compensated.

Then came the advent of Fixed Recoverable Costs, such that Fast Track claims (the bread and butter of claimant firms) only attract modest costs, the formula being applied depending on the point reached by the time the case concludes. A claimant lawyer can spend more time if he wants, but he will have to show that the case is exceptional if he is to exceed the limited costs recoverable.

More recently, section 57 of the Criminal Justice and Courts Act 2015 then required the court to dismiss the entirety of a claim, including the genuine aspects, if it could be shown, *on the balance of probability*, that the claimant has been fundamentally dishonest in relation to the primary claim or a related claim, unless satisfied that the claimant would suffer substantial injustice if the claim were dismissed.

Such threats might mean that a claimant's lawyers will not proceed because of the risks, but even if the claimant discontinues his claim, the defendant can seek to reopen the matter to argue, often in the absence of the claimant, that the claim was clearly dishonest (as evidenced by the fact that the claimant "did not want to pursue it"), so that he can be pursued for costs and his QOCS protection can be set aside.

The high number of reported cases of fundamental dishonesty, setting aside of discontinuances, removal of QOCS protection and committals for contempt is held up as evidence that the system is riddled with corrupt cases. There is some legitimacy to the defendants' position, but the playing field is hardly balanced. The claimant, who can only recover fixed costs even if he wins, is simply not in a position to counter an insurance company who, simply by raising an allegation of dishonesty or questioning the veracity of the claim in some other way, can create so much work for the claimant's solicitors that they are forced to abandon the case.

There are a modest number of reported cases where such allegations (which can have devastating effects on those so accused) are nevertheless fought and dismissed, but, again, the risk of not getting paid forces all but the most determined lawyers away from cases, irrespective of the merits. There may even be cases where a fundamentally dishonest claimant has somehow availed himself of the exception to the rule imposed by section 57, but they are not obvious.

Finally, in a last desperate attempt to kill off the entire personal injury industry, the government and the insurance industry have started to target particular types of injury as being subject to tariff awards rather than compensatory ones. Stories of tens of thousands of redundant lawyers are now rife as we move to a forensic dystopia.

Lawyers inevitably hark back to the days when they started through rose-tinted spectacles (surely something has improved in the last 50 years?) but the effect of each of the recent changes has been drastic on the profession as a whole, and the rights of injured people in particular, who, if they cannot show that they have good prospects of success, are unlikely to persuade a lawyer even to look at their case.

So, is there a future? Seriously injured claimants will still need representation, and at the lower end of the spectrum, claims will still be brought, albeit for less compensation and with lower costs. There has to be an objective concern for the quality of the legal profession who work in this field, but that does not appear to be a factor in the approach being taken. Similar problems afflict other parts of the legal profession, particularly those which are publicly funded.

There is, nevertheless, genuine satisfaction to be had, whether acting for an injured person who, but for your involvement and the rule of three for claimants, would be on the scrap heap or for an insurer, defending spurious claims in whichever of the categories posed by the rule of three for defendants. Such is the game that is played out in offices and courts across this country.

CONCLUSION

My hope, in writing this book, is that by setting out a good proportion of the playing field, the reader will, at any given time, have a better chance of appreciating not just where he is, but also where he might prefer to be and how to get there. That does not mean that there are no hazards to be overcome, just that this overview should make them easier to spot.

Praise for On Experts

"He writes as he speaks: He surveys the territory with the advantage of a wealth of experience, richly leavened with a generous helping of personal anecdote, thereby combining authority with accessibility."
– Turner J

"A well-written, comprehensive and engaging account of the issues encountered in being a medical expert ... clearly important and worthy of wider dissemination"
– Dr Hector Chinoy, PhD FRCP, Senior Lecturer & Honorary Consultant Rheumatologist, Salford Royal NHS Foundation Trust

"Clearly informed by extensive practical experience ... this is a book that is needed and should be purchased by lawyers and anyone who is thinking of giving 'expert' evidence"
– Gordon Exall, Barrister, Zenith Chambers, Leeds & Hardwicke Building, London, Author of Civil Litigation Brief blog

"Eloquently explains a number of complex issues relating to pitfalls in civil expert evidence ... all experts will benefit from the contents of this book when honestly reflecting on their own practises"
– Peter Etherington, Forensic Engineer, George Parkinson Ltd

"Should be used as a teaching guide for new judges, let alone Counsel, litigation solicitors and experts"
– Timothy Gray, District Judge, St Helens County Court

Praise for An Introduction To Personal Injury Law

"A very fine over-view of this important area ... explaining in lucid terms, to professional and lay clients alike, the relevant underlying principles and the practical nuts and bolts of personal injury law... a splendid vade mecum for those seeking a true introduction to this field."
– Stewart J

"A comprehensive, easy to read, guide to personal injury claims with a wealth of information to assist even the most experienced practitioner."
- Lesley Graham, Past President, CILEx

"Aided by the author's nuggets of wisdom and practical experience ... this is a useful tool in every litigator's armoury"
– Gordon Exall, Barrister, Zenith Chambers, Leeds & Hardwicke Building, London, Author of Civil Litigation Brief blog

"In this impressive yet concise work, the author has successfully achieved the ambitious twin aims of clearly communicating practical knowledge drawn from specialist experience, and conveying to the reader a wider understanding of the broader issues and drivers of behaviour in personal injury disputes. Doing so with an accessible style and pragmatic approach is a real achievement. I have no doubt that this work will soon become an immensely valuable go-to resource for anyone needing to understand quickly the important issues in this complex field."
- John Bates, Senior Tort Lecturer, Northumbria University

MORE BOOKS BY LAW BRIEF PUBLISHING

'On Experts: CPR35 for Lawyers and Experts' by David Boyle
'Ellis and Kevan on Credit Hire, 5th Edition' by Aidan Ellis & Tim Kevan
'RTA Allegations of Fraud in a Post-Jackson Era: The Handbook, 2nd Edition' by Andrew Mckie
'A Practical Guide to Holiday Sickness Claims' by Andrew Mckie & Ian Skeate
'RTA Personal Injury Claims: A Practical Guide Post-Jackson' by Andrew Mckie
'A Practical Guide to Claims Arising From Accidents Abroad and Travel Claims' by Andrew Mckie & Ian Skeate
'A Practical Guide to Claims Arising from Fatal Accidents' by James Patience
'A Practical Approach to Clinical Negligence Post-Jackson' by Geoffrey Simpson-Scott
'A Practical Guide to Personal Injury Trusts' by Alan Robinson
'Occupiers, Highways and Defective Premises Claims: A Practical Guide Post-Jackson' by Andrew Mckie
'Employers' Liability Claims: A Practical Guide Post-Jackson' by Andrew Mckie
'A Practical Guide to Subtle Brain Injury Claims' by Pankaj Madan
'A Practical Guide to Chronic Pain Claims' by Pankaj Madan

'The Law of Driverless Cars: An Introduction' by Alex Glassbrook
'A Practical Guide to Costs in Personal Injury Cases' by Matthew Hoe
'A Practical Guide to Alternative Dispute Resolution in Personal Injury Claims – Getting the Most Out of ADR Post-Jackson' by Peter Causton, Nichola Evans, James Arrowsmith
'A Practical Guide to Personal Injuries in Sport' by Adam Walker & Patricia Leonard
'A Practical Guide to Marketing for Lawyers' by Catherine Bailey & Jennet Ingram
'Baby Steps: A Guide to Maternity Leave and Maternity Pay' by Leah Waller
'The Queen's Counsel Lawyer's Omnibus: 20 Years of Cartoons from the Times 1993-2013' by Alex Steuart Williams

These books and more are available to order online direct from the publisher at www.lawbriefpublishing.com, where you can also read free sample chapters. For any queries, contact us on 0844 587 2383 or mail@lawbriefpublishing.com.

Our books are also usually in stock at www.amazon.co.uk with free next day delivery for Prime members, and at good legal bookshops such as Hammicks and Wildy & Sons.

We are regularly launching new books in our series of practical day-to-day practitioners' guides. Visit our website and join our free newsletter to be kept informed.